how to Collect *a* Life

ELIZABETH HUDSON

artwork by Douglas Hoover

copyright © 2016 by *Our State* magazine.
All rights reserved.
Published by *Our State* magazine, Mann Media, Inc.
PO Box 4552, Greensboro, NC 27404
(800) 948-1409 | ourstate.com
Printed in the United States by R.R. Donnelley

No part of this book may be used or reproduced
in any manner without written permission.

DESIGN DIRECTOR: Claudia Royston
ART DIRECTOR: Jason Chenier
ART COORDINATOR: Hannah Wright

Library of Congress Control Number: 2016909266

table *of* contents

IT WAS A GOOD LUNCH ... 4
SPRING CLEAN ... 6
NO OCEAN IN THE MOUNTAINS ... 8
HEY, GOOD LOOKIN' ... 12
A SILENT SALUTE ... 14
WHAT YOU CAN'T SEE ... 16
HOW LOVELY IT WAS ... 20
AND DANCE BY THE LIGHT OF THE MOON ... 22
MAGIC OF THE MOVIES ... 24
SEA CHANGE ... 28
SCENT OF THE SOUTH ... 30
WHAT THESE WORDS CAN DO ... 32
WHEN LIFE WAS SO TENDER ... 36
FULL SERVICE ... 38
ANIMAL RESCUE ... 40
EASY LISTENING ... 44
A WISH FOR CHRISTMAS ... 46
MIDSUMMER CLASSIC ... 48

BEAUTY IS IN THE EYE	52
FROM THE BOOTH	54
THE LANGUAGE OF FLOWERS	56
IN SEARCH OF SAFE PLACES	60
ONE DAY IN MAY	62
LEAVING A MARK	64
ONE OF US	68
PEACE IN THE VALLEY	70
SOMETHING IN THE AIR	72
OUR SEASON OF SO MUCH	76
CHANGE GONNA COME	78
EVERYBODY TALKS ABOUT IT	80
A YEAR OF FIRSTS	84
THE PERFECT PLATE	86
BESIDE THE STILL WATERS	88
HOW TO COLLECT A LIFE	92
GLASS HALF FULL	94

it was a Good Lunch

I n the 1940s, when the bell rang for lunch, the boys and girls at Coleridge School reached beneath their desks and pulled out their lunch bags, brown paper sacks that held whatever their moms put in there that morning.

Some bags held tins of sardines. Vienna sausages. Pork and beans.

My dad's bag held the same thing every day: a potted-meat sandwich on white bread and a baked sweet potato that he peeled and ate like a banana.

He never complained. It was a good lunch.

When he got a little older, he left school at lunchtime. Crossed the road and jumped the creek with the other boys to get to Martin's Store, where he ordered a fried bologna sandwich at the counter. Everyone sat on benches in front of Martin's and unwrapped their fried bolognas from waxed paper and ate until they could hear the bell clang. Then they crossed back with just enough time to run into the basement at the schoolhouse. There was refrigeration in the basement, including a big metal cooler that was stocked to the rim with Eskimo Pies. Ten cents. Everybody bought one.

IN THE 1950S, MY MOTHER ATE A HOT lunch — 25 cents — every day in the

Nathanael Greene School cafeteria, part of the National School Lunch Program implemented by President Truman in 1946. She had country-style steak. Creamed corn. Macaroni and cheese and pinto beans and no-bake chocolate-oatmeal cookies.

The cafeteria ladies fixed the children's plates and handed them over on a tray — you didn't get to choose, but no one ever complained. It was a good lunch.

Frances Holt was the cafeteria manager then; when she retired, she opened a restaurant in Liberty called Fran's Front Porch. She served the same dishes those schoolchildren remembered and loved and wanted to keep eating. That restaurant has closed now, and I think of all the generations who will never taste a dinner at Fran's; or a hot lunch, circa 1950s, at the Nathanael Greene cafeteria; or a fried-bologna-and-mustard sandwich while sitting outside a store.

IN THE 1970S, MY MOTHER PACKED MY lunchbox with the same sandwich every day: banana-and-mayonnaise. No choice. I got a tin of potato sticks and an aluminum can of chocolate pudding. I remember pulling the metal lid off the pudding and licking the back of it, and I shudder at the thought now: How is it that I didn't cut my tongue on the metal?

Our lunchboxes were metal, too. The boys had The Six Million Dollar Man and Hong Kong Phooey. I had Holly Hobbie, Peanuts, and Scooby Doo, a new one every year, until fourth grade, when we moved to the country and I went to Farmer School and no longer needed a lunchbox because we had a cafeteria, like the one my mom had. Chicken pie and spaghetti and paper cups of chocolate ice cream that we scooped with tiny wooden paddles.

I miss those meals. I miss being handed a tray of something, no choices. I miss my grandmother's fried chicken. I miss the foot-long hot dogs my dad made in his sandwich shop on Fayetteville Street in Asheboro. The fried egg my grandfather made in his small egg pan every morning. My dad says he's never seen a man so excited to go to bed at night because he had an egg to look forward to eating in the morning.

At lunchtime now, I go check on my mom at home. She eats the same sandwich every day. I'll make you one, too, she says.

She lays down four pieces of bread — Merita, the same kind she's been buying for 50 years — and spreads Hellmann's on the bread. This is a shock. Don't we eat Duke's? All those years, I never knew. I watch her slice bananas into rounds, flipping them over her finger onto the bread. She mashes the bread down lightly with the palm of her hand.

We sit across from each other at the table, and I watch her pick up her sandwich and bite into it.

Isn't this good, she says. She means it.

Yes, I say. Thank you. It's a really good lunch. *Os*

Spring Clean

Went to check on my mama the other day and found her in the kitchen, sweeping the floor, as usual. She was wearing my dad's old L.L. Bean moccasins, the ones with the smooth soles, the ones he wore every day, and I didn't want to interrupt so I sat at the kitchen table and watched her, listening to those shoes soft-shuffle behind the switch-switch of her broom.

And because I wondered what was going through her mind when she swept — she does this several times a day, and has for as long as I can remember — I asked her, "How long you been sweeping, Mom?" and she looked up and said just a few minutes, and I said, "No, I mean how long in your life?"

And she said, "Since I was 6 years old."

SIXTY YEARS AGO, MY MOTHER SPENT most of her time at her grandmother's house in Julian, a two-story, six-room farmhouse with three porches: a great, wide front porch 40 feet long, a side porch, and a back porch.

The front porch was scattered with stray ladder-backs and rockers; nothing matched. My mother's grandfather —she called him Papaw — brought in wood for the kitchen cookstove through the side porch and carted in water from the well. A wringer washing machine stood on the back porch.

Those porches were where everybody congregated, either for work or for socializing.

Back then, nobody traveled far. Papaw walked to the store for groceries. Neighbors came over and sat. My mom and her grandmother — Granny — cut up watermelon on those porches, and they shelled butter beans and peas out there, too, enamelware pails anchored between their knees, peas rat-a-tatting into them.

Twice a day, morning and night, Granny took her broom to the porches. She swept down the front porch first, starting at the eaves and sweeping out spiderwebs, breaking up dirt daubers' nests, then flipped over all the chairs and swept the undersides and slats, straightening them back up, and finally swept the floor itself.

My mother, a little girl then, watched Granny's every motion, and before long, she picked up a broom and started sweeping, too, and since then, I've known her to sweep every day, all these years — the crumbs from the crust of a pie after my dad couldn't wait to cut a slice, carrying his piece on a paper plate to the den to eat in front of the television on the nights Carolina was playing; the dog hair shed from our old beagle, Muffin, after a morning of warming her stiff legs in the sun by the front door; eraser shavings brushed onto the floor on the nights I sat at the dining table and cried because I couldn't understand my math homework; sawdust my dad tracked in after a day in the garage building his birdhouses, and, later, the birdseed that found its way past the threshold after he'd filled up the seven feeders in the backyard; the clods of red dirt that came off his shoes after planting tomatoes; the wisps of his hair — before they married, she'd gone to beauty school, and for 45 years, my dad never had anyone cut his hair but her.

I watch my mom sweep a floor that has less traffic now, less activity, but she keeps going. She sweeps the corners, her broom clearing the cobwebs and brushing away the gauze of memory, and I am amazed and grateful that such a small task can do so much to make everything feel so fresh and bright. **OS**

No Ocean
in the
Mountains

A lesson in learning to love a landscape.

In 1988, I slapped an Appalachian State University sticker on the rear window of my car and headed west to the mountains.

I drove away from my home in Randolph County, down U.S. Highway 64, and past the Uwharries, which, until my college years, had been the highest peaks I'd ever seen.

On move-in day, I met my roommate, who was from Raleigh and had already claimed her side of the room and covered our cinder-block walls with *Dirty Dancing* posters. We were strangers trying to make the best of an unfamiliar place, and here's what I did:

I bought the sweatshirts. I ate in the cafeteria. And in the Gold Room. And in the Sweet Shop. I piled seven people in my car and drove to the top of Howard's Knob. I tried to ski. I joined the Student Government Association, as a freshman representative. I went to my first football game — the Mountaineers played the Citadel Bulldogs — and the stadium was a sea of black and gold.

Except there was no sea here at all.

There is no ocean in the mountains, and I found myself wondering how I ended up in a place like this when what I preferred was flat land, warm weather, salt breezes. A landscape that didn't rise and didn't fall.

That year in Boone, it snowed in October. It kept on snowing. The snow piled up. Falling and rising.

It was cold, and I was lonely.

I felt the weight of all that snow, and I felt the weight of all those mountains, pushing down on me, pushing the breath out of me, pushing the life out of me.

Six months later, hanging my head in shame, I packed my car up and came home. I left the mountains, and it was a long time before I went back.

Years later, I took a job here, at *Our State*, and I went to Asheville for the magazine's annual Best of Our State event. I sat on the terrace at the Grove Park Inn, and I noticed, for the first time, how the mountains sparkled. I saw the evening lights of Asheville in the distance. I saw more stars in the sky than I'd ever seen in my life.

Soon after, I started going other places in western North Carolina. I followed a steep spiral in Taylorsville and found a man selling the best mountain apples I've ever tasted; I drove far out to Brasstown and learned how to pluck the strings of a dulcimer; I sat on the back of a truck bed and watched for the Brown Mountain Lights near Morganton; I went to Little Switzerland and ate a smoked trout BLT; and I drove Railroad Grade Road in Ashe County and stopped my car to let a family of wild turkeys cross in front of me.

> **I saw more stars in the sky than I'd ever seen in my life.**

It took a long time for them to get across — they were in no hurry — and as I rolled down the window and listened to the burble of the New River, I realized neither was I.

After 25 years, I'd made peace with these mountains, pulled closer by time and distance.

NOT LONG AGO, I TRAVELED 3,315 FEET into the sky, to a place called Wildacres, a retreat center on the top of Pompey's Knob near the Blue Ridge Parkway. I spent a week in an isolated mountain cabin with no phone service, television, or Internet access.

During the day, I worked. At night, I sat outside and watched the sky turn from purple to black, stars popping. I tuned the small radio in the cabin to WNCW out of Spindale and listened to Underhill Rose and Earl Scruggs and the Foggy Mountain Boys. I listened to Boone Creek sing the truth about drifting too far from the shore.

While I was at Wildacres, so was a world-class bassoon camp. Every day at 4 p.m., bassoonists from symphonies all over the United States gathered for a recital, and I walked up the hill from my cabin to listen to them practice. They played Vivaldi and Mozart and Bach, and I had never heard sounds like this before, undulating waves emanating from their instruments. Like an ocean in the mountains. Rising and falling.

As I listened, I realized what I'd missed so many years ago, before I understood that, in this life, there are rises and there are falls. And there are places in this state that can shoulder all of that, strong places that aren't pushing us down at all but lifting us up.

I looked around at the hills, and I whispered a thank-you. It was as if they whispered back, "Don't worry. We weren't going anywhere." *OS*

Hey, Good Lookin'

It was the 1970s, but my grandmother still had a collection of *Life* magazines from the '40s and '50s. She kept them in a dress box under the bed, and in the afternoon, when she took her nap, I'd crawl under the bed and pull that box out.

Those magazines smelled good — musty and smoky and newspapery — and I loved turning their delicate pages and looking at the images of the women in those old photographs who stared back at me. I imagined myself living in that time period, and I pulled clothes out of my grandmother's closet — her fitted suits from when she worked in the Randolph County tax department in the '50s; her cocktail dresses for dinners with my grandfather at Pinewood Country Club — and I dressed myself up, trying to mimic Dorian Leigh in her elbow-length satin gloves and Lena Horne in her gauzy scarves and pretty models in cat-eye glasses. My final touch was a swipe of my grandmother's red lipstick.

She kept her cosmetics in the top drawer of the dresser in her bedroom. Coty Airspun face powder in a gold hatbox container. A pink glass jar of Olay night cream. Gold torpedo tubes of lipstick: Revlon's Fire and Ice. Cherries in the Snow. Love That Red.

Revlon introduced its line of those red lipsticks in the early 1950s, perhaps as a Technicolor antidote to the monochromatic war years. My grandmother found her signature color — Love That Red — and stayed loyal to it for the rest of her life.

At the Duke Homestead State Historic Site in Durham, I saw that lipstick again.

I WAS THERE FOR THE ANNUAL PORK, Pickles, and Peanuts festival, which concludes with a mock 1940s-style pageant to select the Tobacco Queen. In tobacco's heyday, a harvest festival was held at the opening of tobacco auction season. Tobacco queen contests were intended to boost tobacco sales, and I guess it worked.

On this day at Duke Homestead, six "contestants" (actually student interns at the site) — sashed as Miss Salisbury, Miss Apex, Miss Bahama, Miss Chapel Hill, Miss Durham, and Miss Raleigh — wore 1940s and '50s attire and performed a skit in front of an audience of festivalgoers. One girl clogged; another performed a hula dance to "Little Brown Gal."

And all of them wore red lipstick. Fire and Ice. Cherries in the Snow. Love That Red.

Then I heard the music. Before the pageant started, the Malpass Brothers, a family band from Goldsboro, took the stage. I sat under a tent and ate a barbecue sandwich wrapped in white paper. I listened as Christopher and Taylor Malpass sang Ernest Tubb and Tom T. Hall. They played so many old songs — Marty Robbins's "Devil Woman," Elvis's "CC Rider," and Merle Haggard's "That's the Way It Was in '51," — but the crowd really went crazy when the band broke out into a rendition of "Hey, Good Lookin'."

Hank Williams's song came out in '51, yet everyone in the audience — this modern audience — knew the lyrics. I watched as the people under the tent stood up and set their paper bags of boiled peanuts in their chairs and started swaying and clapping and singing. *There's soda pop and the dancing's free, so if you wanna have fun come along with me.*

On that day, the past burst through to the present. And for a second, it wasn't hard to imagine that if I turned around, I'd see my grandmother sitting there, too, right behind me, looking exactly like those girls on the stage, her hair pin-curled and her smile rimmed in that red lipstick. Love That Red.

It makes me happy to know that, in North Carolina, we have places like this, where the colorless veil of memory lifts, and the past stares back at us, all dressed up and looking every bit as beautiful as we remember. *Os*

A Silent Salute

We carry things inside us that others can't see.

When I was in the fourth grade, I got hit by a car as I was going back to my grandmother's after playing in a park two blocks away from her house.

I didn't see the car coming fast over the hill. The driver, a high school student in his mother's sedan, was a baseball player. He was on his way to an American Legion ball game, and he was in a hurry.

He didn't see the little girl crossing the street.

The impact threw me up in the air and knocked my glasses off my face. I landed 20 feet down the hill, my T-shirt peeled away from my back, a layer of skin scrubbed away.

There were a lot of people standing over me. I remember a woman saying — she may have been screaming — "I'm a nurse; we need an ambulance."

I didn't want to get in an ambulance, so I stood, somehow, and walked the two blocks to my grandmother's house.

My mother came. The police came. The kid who hit me came. Everyone was scared.

I went to the hospital anyway, got bandaged up, and eventually healed, except for an indention in my right hip. It's still there. You'd never notice it.

The kid who hit me was young, 17 years old. Nobody pressed any charges; it was an accident. That kid would be in his 50s now, and I wonder if he ever had children. I wonder if he ever told them what happened. I know he carries with him the horror of hitting a little girl, and even though she turned out fine, that's enough for anyone to have to hold on to.

You might think that there's no connection between the story I just told you and the one I'm about to tell you, but here's why I was reminded of that day.

Last month, I went to Washington, D.C., to participate in the North Carolina Business and Economic Development Summit. I was there to talk about the state, and *Our State*, and it was humbling to stand on Capitol Hill and see our American flag flying atop the building, and to think about all the things — many of which we'll never know — that have happened in our history to keep us all walking free. It made me hold my head high.

In one of the meetings, I listened to a four-star general in the U.S. Marine Corps speak about the enormous contribution of North Carolina's military and the profound effect our bases, and the training that happens here, have had on the nation, on the world.

I had the stories from our November issue, a special veterans issue, fresh in my head, so, at the break, I leaned over and spoke to the man sitting beside me, a businessman named David McLamb who had come up from Laurinburg.

He said that he grew up in Fayetteville in the '60s.

He said then, as now, the military presence was tremendous.

He said his draft number was 179. They were going to 190.

David told me about gathering in the high school gymnasium, with so many other boys, for the draft call. They all listened, hearts pounding, hoping, praying, that it wouldn't be their number, that it wouldn't be their number, that it wouldn't be their number.

He said when someone's number came up, the boy spat out a profanity, got up, and left the room. Eventually, David's number was called.

He teared up when he was talking to me. I saw the welling in his eyes as he remembered something I'll never know, something he carries deep inside him, like all veterans do.

Like all humans do.

I thought about my accident as an 8-year-old child; I thought about the 17-year-old kid; I thought about all the people — our neighbors, coworkers, friends, brothers, sons, fathers — who carry scars others can't see. About how we go on anyway, with courage, with strength, with our heads held high.

Maybe, in an embrace of humanity, we all ought to give each other a nod.

A handshake.

A hug.

A silent salute to the burdens we bear. *Os*

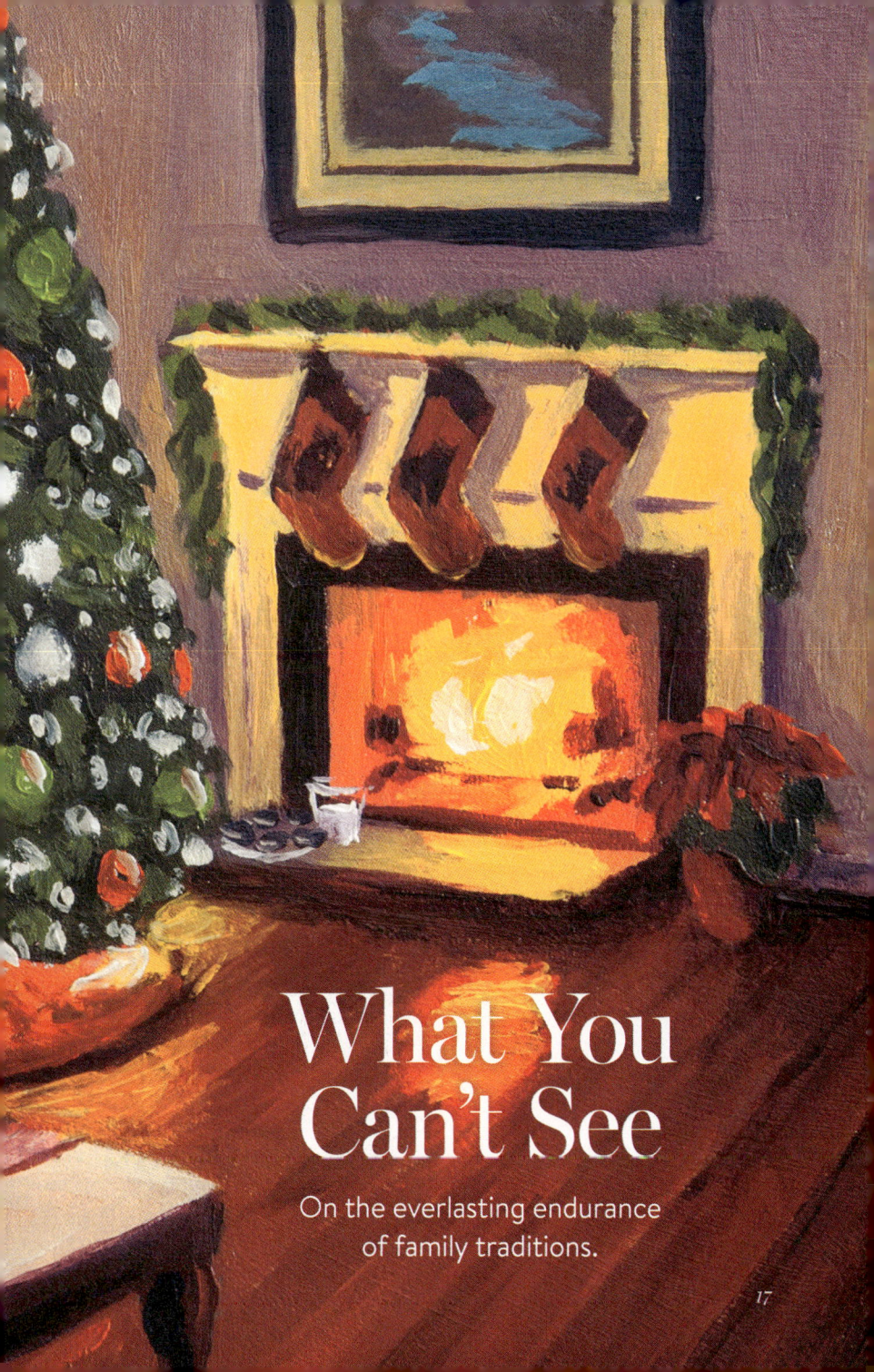

What You Can't See

On the everlasting endurance of family traditions.

Five Oreo cookies. In my house, that's what Santa Claus preferred, his favorite cookie; I know this because my dad told me it was so.

On Christmas Eve, I spread a circle of Oreos on a plate and set it on our brick fireplace hearth next to a full glass of milk. And I went to bed.

In the morning, before I allowed myself to look at the tree, before I allowed myself to peek inside the stockings, before I allowed myself to wake up my parents and wait for them to pour coffee, I checked the plate.

It was a gift itself — and a relief — to see the crumbs, the empty glass with a milk ring in the bottom, evidence — proof — that Santa had indeed come to the Hudson household, that he had not forgotten us this year after all.

Those Christmas mornings were as happy as anything I can remember. We took our places — Dad in his chair, Mom in her chair, me on the floor, the same positions every year — and started with our stockings.

One at a time, each of us dug in. My dad pulled out his can of Barbasol shaving cream; my mom pulled out a pair of leather gloves; and I pulled out a bag of Bazooka Joe bubble gum. The items were the same every year, a tradition born through repetition. So much stays the same at Christmas.

Except, of course, it doesn't.

MY PARENTS CELEBRATED THEIR FIRST Christmas as a married couple in 1969.

That year, the two of them went to Kmart on North Main Street in High Point and bought a six-foot-tall artificial tree, reams of plastic greenery and garlands, and a cartful of multicolored, mercury-glass ornaments.

They decorated their small house on Eastchester Drive and trimmed their new tree and sat together on the sofa, admiring the glow of the lights, mentally recording the placement of the ornaments so they could duplicate it the next year, and every year after that.

When my parents moved to Asheboro in 1972 with me, a 2-year-old, in tow, they carted those decorations with us. And when we moved to

18 WHAT YOU CAN'T SEE

Farmer seven years later, those same Christmas decorations were some of the first things to make it onto the moving truck.

That first year in our new house, my mother hammered nails in the new barnwood walls in our den. She put up a wooden NOEL and her painted candy canes, gifts from friends who were regular customers so many years ago in her crafts shop. She hung her collection of pewter ornaments on a wreath that the girls who worked for her went in together to buy; she hung my framed letter to Santa Claus from 1976. On the coffee table, she displayed a collection of hand-painted Santa Clauses from her best friend and, in a basket, my dad's collection of illustrated Christmas books from his childhood. She draped garlands — the same garlands from that Kmart in High Point — on the mantel and looped our stockings onto their nails.

My grandmother made those stockings, painstakingly needlepointing every stitch, including our names. There's a colorful train on my dad's stocking. My mom's shows leaping reindeer, and mine has a Raggedy Ann on the front.

My grandmother is no longer here — it's been 20 years now — but when those stockings are on display, they are evidence — proof — that she was.

This year, there's a For Sale sign in the front yard of the house. My parents have put many of their belongings in storage, waiting for the day when the real estate agent says it's time to go.

On Christmas morning, we'll sit together like we've done for 35 years, our small family circle, surrounded by everything in the same place.

We'll start with the stockings.

Barbasol.

Gloves.

Bubble gum.

I'll look around at everything, mentally recording the placement of it all so that I won't ever forget it: the decorations on the walls, the stockings on the mantel, my mom and dad in their chairs, drinking coffee and watching the glow of the lights.

It's becoming so clear to me that real gifts aren't the ones under the tree. *Os*

19

How Lovely *It Was*

Before I was old enough for midnight movies or grown-up parties or champagne dinners, I spent every New Year's Eve with my grandmother.

After supper — sweet tea, no champagne — the two of us pushed our chairs back from the table, hooked our arms together, and escorted each other to the living room, where we climbed onto the bench in front of her Lowrey Magic Genie electronic organ.

We sat side by side and worked our way through the "Fun With the Lowrey Organ" songbook, singing "Home on the Range" and "Good Night Ladies" and "Aloha 'Oe." While my grandmother played and worked the foot pedals, my job was to adjust the accompaniment tabs to change the rhythm from country western to bossa nova to Hawaiian guitar.

It was amazing to me how you could affect the sound of a song just by changing its background rhythm.

We played for hours at that organ, and, at some point, I stopped pressing the accompaniment buttons and dropped my hands to my lap and just listened. My grandmother had a beautiful alto voice, soothing and sweet, and when my energy started to wane, she shifted to quieter pieces and sang them directly to me.

One of my favorite songs was "Thanks for the Memory." It was from an old, black-and-white movie that my grandmother loved. There were a lot of verses in the song, and I didn't understand most of the lines — "crap games on the floor, nights in Singapore" — but I loved the wink she gave me when she sang "moments on the Hudson River Line," drawing out the emphasis on our last name.

By the end of the song, her voice started to lose its steadiness, and I knew it was time to stop. She slid us back from the organ, stood up, and, once again, extended her elbow to me. I hooked my arm into hers, and we escorted each other to the den, as if we were leaving a grand ballroom.

I think about how we walked, that motion now familiar in other ways, too. It was the same arm-in-arm gesture my mother offered when, years later, she helped my grandmother from her bed to the bathroom; it was the same one my father offered when he walked with me, finally a grown-up, down the aisle of the church at her funeral. I'm not sure which one of us was holding up the other.

Toward the end of our New Year's Eve night, I changed into my pajamas and my grandmother slipped on her pink robe and we settled into her chair to watch Guy Lombardo's, and later, Dick Clark's New Year's Eve special. When I got sleepy and my head drooped, she tickled me until I started laughing. It was enough to help me make it to midnight, and when we had five minutes to spare, my grandmother went to the dining room for two jelly glasses and a bottle of Canada Dry ginger ale. We turned off all the lights and watched the ticker on the television and then, all of a sudden, everything moved so fast and, sensing the urgency of it all, we jumped up for the countdown — ten, nine, eight — and stepped closer to the television and lifted our glasses and shouted, "Happy New Year!" exactly the way the crowd dressed in ball gowns and tuxedos in Times Square did, and then, just like that, a new number flashed on the screen and "Auld Lang Syne" started playing in the background, a familiar song providing accompaniment to whatever it was that might come next. *Os*

and Dance *by the* Light *of the* Moon

The newspaper hits my driveway at 5 a.m. It's still dark outside, but this is when my day begins. It's odd to think of a new day, of morning, as starting in the dark.

Every morning, although it looks like evening when I go out to get my newspaper, I look up.

I take a few deliberate minutes, before I skitter back into the house, to look up at the sky and find the stars. To anchor my gaze on the moon.

My house faces east. When I go to bed, I often see the moon high above my front yard; by the early morning, the moon has migrated to the western sky, where eventually it sets, behind my house.

Every morning, when I'm standing outside in my slippered feet in the dark, I'm comforted by the constancy of the moon and the stars up there in their rightful place, by the knowledge that these celestial bodies have inhabited their positions in the sky for a long, long time. When I look up, I can find what I'm looking for.

I've always been curious about the Earth, but more so, I've always been curious about whatever is beyond the Earth. If you came to my house, you'd see my collection of globes. I started collecting them when I was in college, my interest spurred on by geography and earth science classes. My favorite globe, though, isn't an Earth globe at all.

It's a moon globe.

The thing has some years on it — it was manufactured in the early 1960s, a tribute to the space race and our collective dream of exploring beyond our terrestrial borders. It's got some wear on it, too. It's made of tin, and there are a few cratered dents and pockmarks. Kind of like the actual moon, I suppose. Nothing stays new forever.

TWO MONTHS AGO, MY PARENTS SOLD their house, the one they've lived in nearly all my life, the home where I grew up. They moved to a small townhome about a half-mile from me.

Think of it. So many years spent in one place. And then, in the span of one day, movers came and backed a 26-foot truck into the driveway and filled the truck with furniture and mattresses and lamps and boxes full of dishes and clothing and photos, and then the movers drove away, and that was that.

My parents woke up one morning in the house they've known for a long, long time; they went to sleep that night somewhere entirely different. Overnight, their view changed.

They're getting settled now in their new place. On their third night, I took them out to eat. My dad doesn't drive anymore, and my mother doesn't drive at night. Back at their old place in Asheboro, they never went out to eat in the evening because they would've had to drive home in the dark.

We headed down Elm Street toward downtown Greensboro, and my mother craned her neck to look up through the windshield. "Phil!" she said to my dad. "Look at these big buildings!" She kept saying it over and over. The tallest building in downtown Greensboro is the old Jefferson Standard Building, Lincoln Financial now. At a little more than 200 feet, it's no match for other cities' skyscrapers. But that night, it was beautiful, nearly every window glowing with so much warm light from within.

Back in their new place, my parents are still unpacking. I watch as they pull familiar things from the boxes — my mom's pottery dishes; wooden whirligigs; an antique tin horse, three feet tall, that stood, for as long as I can remember, in the den in the old house.

It's not easy navigating a new course.

My parents' new living room, though, faces east. On most nights, they'll be able to see the moon rise. I'll bet it'll be bright. I'll bet it'll be beautiful. I'll bet it'll light up the whole house, pulling everything away from the shadows, out of the dark. *O_S*

Magic of the Movies

The exhilaration of recording life through a lens.

When my dad went off to college at UNC in the 1950s, his friends made fun of him the first time he suggested they go to the "picture show." That's all he'd ever heard the movies called when he was growing up in the small town of Coleridge, and his friends laughed at him for being so country.

This year, the *Los Angeles Times* reported that Paramount Pictures stopped releasing movies on film. From now on, distribution will be digital. Nothing to hold on to. No reel to load. Nothing to thread into a hulking 35-millimeter projector.

It won't affect how we see movies — "picture shows" — in a theater. To us, the audience, those pictures will look the same on the screen — but do you know what this means? It means we can no longer legitimately call them "films."

WHEN I WAS 10 YEARS OLD, I GOT A handheld Canon Super 8 movie camera for a birthday present. For months, I walked around with the rubber eyecup of the camera pressed against my glasses, and I aimed that thing everywhere — at the birds on the feeder in the backyard, at my mom while she washed dishes and folded laundry, at my dad drinking coffee at the kitchen table. With no real storyline to shoot, I recorded the mundane details of my family's day.

That camera, though, fueled for me a lifelong passion for movies — not just going to them but also a love for how they're made. In high school, I subscribed to moviemaking magazines, and when I was in college, I got a job in a video store. We played movies on a loop all day in the store, and after work, I went to midnight screenings at the Terrace and the Janus, fantastic independent movie theaters in Greensboro. In fact, when the Janus opened in the late '60s, it was the only two-screen theater between Washington, D.C., and Atlanta, Georgia.

For years, I saw nearly every movie that came to those theaters. I was one of the first in line on opening night of *The Last of the Mohicans*; I remember the amped-up adrenaline of the audience watching *Days of Thunder*. All of us in our seats in the darkened theater were answering the universal call of the movies: a chance to escape from the commonplace of our own lives; two hours of romance and action and drama and comedy and animation — storylines that were long ways away from washing dishes and folding laundry and drinking coffee at the kitchen table.

The Terrace and the Janus are no more — Romano's Macaroni Grill restaurant now sits in the spot where I crossed through those red velvet ropes so many times; a multistory First Citizens Bank now sits in the spot that used to house the Janus.

But that's the beauty of movie theaters — long after they're gone, you can still remember what they held. And that's the beauty of movies, too. Long after the show is over, you still remember the story.

I HAVEN'T SEEN THOSE REELS FROM MY Super 8 camera in many decades, but I know what's on them: There are frames of me walking up the staircase of our old house, dressed in my pajamas and proudly holding out my palm with a tooth in it; I'm sure I must've put it under my pillow when I got to my bedroom. There are other scenes, too: a five-minute stretch of green trees and blurry mountains shot from a car window on a drive along the Blue Ridge Parkway. My grandmother and grandfather standing beneath a sprig of mistletoe that I Scotch-taped to the door casing in their kitchen; when they realize I'm filming them, they laugh and lean in to kiss each other. And there's a scene of my childhood dog, circling, circling, to find a warm spot in the sunshine beneath a window in our old house.

There's something about that particular scene that makes me so happy — the way her little body curls into a C, the way she tucks her nose beneath her leg. My camera didn't record sound, and yet, I am sure I can hear her toenails tapping on the hardwoods; I am sure I can hear her breathing, softly snoring, on the floor.

Those movies, simple as they were, made us stars in our lives. When I think of these scenes now, they're the opposite of mundane. They're majestic. *Os*

Sea Change

At Ocean Isle Beach, there are things that you might not expect to encounter, like the 11 varieties of palm trees that rise up from The Winds resort, and the sticky ribs and Jamaican fried plantains at the little yellow Sugar Shack, and that just out to sea, not all that far from where you might be standing in the surf, where the backwash drops your heels lower and lower, swims Mary Lee, a 16-foot-long, 3,456-pound great white shark.

Mary Lee might be 20 years old; she might be 70 years old. We don't know how long she's been swimming here — there's no way to measure the age of a living shark — but we know she likes these waters. She was tagged — meaning a satellite chip was implanted in her dorsal fin, thereby tracking her location with a "ping" anytime that fin breaks the water — by marine researchers in 2012. Since then, she's traveled more than 15,000 miles, swimming constantly, up and down the Eastern Seaboard, moving, the way all sharks must continuously keep moving, to keep herself alive.

She's been near Sunset Beach. She skirted Wrightsville Beach and Emerald Isle, and once, she made her way into Pamlico Sound and crossed Ocracoke Inlet.

At Ocean Isle, she pinged, which meant she was nearby, and everyone snapped to attention. We tracked her movements with GPS apps on our phones; the local news reported her whereabouts; and I clinked bottles with a guy at the pool — I'm not kidding, he was drinking a Landshark beer — in tribute when we heard Mary Lee had surfaced briefly, that she'd come back, although for how long, none of us could say.

DON'T YOU THINK WE COME TO THE beach because we want to *stop* moving? The road ends, we can't go any farther, we are forced to stop. To finally be still.

We come to the beach because we like to think it doesn't move, either. Or, at least, we try to keep it from moving too much. We put sandbags on our beaches to push the water back; we repeat our visits, coming back year after year, to the same spot, the same beach cottage, the same motel, the same restaurants. Constancy is security.

Our beach is the same as it ever was, we tell ourselves. We can count on jumping waves for hours in Nags Head, because this is a spot where surf conditions are best, have always been best, will always be best, and afterward, wrung out, we order our fried flounder at Owens' or we cast a line from Kure Beach pier or retell the story about our first summer kiss beneath Johnnie Mercer's Pier at Wrightsville — as fleeting a moment if ever there was one, and yet, 20 years later or 70 years later, we can still taste the warmth of summer tan and salt water on our lips, a remnant memory of the unexpected boy who showed up one summer and never reappeared, and we can still remember that moment when everything shifted from childhood to adulthood, and though we know we must continuously keep moving, keep changing, to keep ourselves alive, we still depend on things to remain the same as they ever were, the same as they will always be.

But that's not how it is, is it?

The most practical among us know that of any place in North Carolina, our coast is the most susceptible to change, to impermanence, to fleeting moments.

But still. We come back, and we look for the things we remember, the places we went, maybe long ago. And we go there, to the places where we can let our memories surface. Ping.

I still check to see where Mary Lee is. If she dies, we might not know. She might wash ashore; researchers might retrieve her body. But they might not. I watch for the pings, and I get a shiver of excitement when she surfaces. I'm glad to know that she's still out there, that she hasn't yet disappeared. *OS*

Scent *of the* South

The man who sold me a bag of birdseed at Wild Birds Unlimited told me this: Birds can't smell.

He wanted to make sure I hung my feeder in an obvious place in the yard so the birds could see it. Birds rely on sight, he said, and color is important. It's why hummingbird feeders have bright red bases.

When I refilled my feeder, I thought about what he'd said, and about how I'd never considered that some creatures don't have the same senses as we do.

I stood in my backyard and breathed in, and I caught the smell of woody rosemary and sweet basil growing in pots on my deck; I could smell someone's charcoal grill, lighter fluid diffusing in the air, a summer symbol of how we yearn to be outdoors, to eat, to live, to feel the sunshine, to smell the air.

HERE IN NORTH CAROLINA, SCENT IS A defining part of who we are. Smells are everywhere — clinging to the rafters of old tobacco barns; rising from bundled hay spread across Piedmont fields; hanging in the briny, sea-salt air in Nags Head, in Hatteras, in Wanchese.

What would it be like to have no sense of smell? Think of all you'd miss.

YOU'D MISS THE HONEYED SWEETNESS of Southern magnolia and gardenia, their scents so irresistible that my grandmother clipped stems and brought them inside the house, floating whole blossoms in cut-glass bowls filled with water. The smell permeated the house within minutes, settling over us like some kind of Southern *Wizard of Oz* poppy, and made us sleepy in the afternoon. I remember climbing into my grandmother's chair, wedging my body next to hers, overcome with so many scents — of those magnolias and gardenias mixed with the smell of her own soft skin, lotioned in Rose Milk. When I walk beneath a sprawling magnolia today, I go straight back to that chair. I go straight back to my childhood.

You'd miss the camphorous smell of the balsam fir forests in Dillsboro and Sylva, and you'd miss the perfume of sweet shrub, Carolina allspice, so pronounced in early evenings after the sun has warmed its burgundy skin. You'd miss the smell of an approaching summer thunderstorm and the smell of deep, damp earth when the rain finally falls.

THE FIRST HOUSE I REMEMBER LIVING in was on Salisbury Street in Asheboro. It was a white bungalow with a front porch and a small fireplace, and inside, in the center of the house, a staircase led to the unfinished basement, where the washing machine was.

On wash days, I sat on the basement's wooden stairs so I could be surrounded by that underground smell — organic, musky, moist, but calming, too. That basement smelled like the newsprint paper of my comic books, and I sat on the steps, taking in that smell for the entire length of a wash cycle, until my mother came down to gather up the clothes in the hamper and take them outside to hang on the line. I followed behind and buried my face right into the basket, breathing in as deeply as I could.

You'd miss the delicate, soapy smell of clothes drying outside on a line.

You'd miss wild honeysuckle.

When I walked with my grandmother in the early evenings before supper, we'd catch a whiff of a patch of honeysuckle before we ever saw it, and the smell caused us to whip our heads around, searching. I can't tell you how many of those white-and-yellow blossoms I've plucked in my life — pinching off the green bud, pulling out the plunger and whistling back the sweet nectar, this confection growing wild, its scent so familiar, you never, ever forget it.

Nature returns these scents to us every season; the power of smell is the power of memory.

If we close our eyes and breathe deeply, we can revisit landscapes that exist only in our minds.

Smell brings us back. It can return to us everything we thought we'd lost. *Os*

What These Words Can Do

In praise of the power of a poem

*"Twinkle, twinkle, little star,
How I wonder what you are,
Up above the world so high ..."*

I'll bet I can tell you what just happened. Whether you're 25 or 45 or 75, you just finished the next line in your head. This poem, written more than 200 years ago, is likely one of the first poems you ever heard in your life, probably sung in a rhyming voice by someone who loved you. You responded with a soft smile, a coo of admiration — and then you never forgot it. You carried this poem around with you for the rest of your life.

You passed it on, along with others. Pat-a-Cake. Old MacDonald. There was an old woman who lived in a shoe. You know these verses by heart.

By first grade, you wrote your own verse, scrawling "Roses are red, violets are blue" on a valentine, and maybe you discovered Dr. Seuss. Then came Shel Silverstein, and later, e.e. cummings and Langston Hughes and Robert Frost and William Carlos Williams, and by then, for you, poetry was no longer a treat; it was a requirement.

Poetry reaches beyond our backyards, crosses our borders.

The poems stopped rhyming, and you stopped reading, and that's when the love ended. Poetry got hard. Who knows why he ate those plums in the icebox? Who cares? Do I dare disturb the universe?

Then comes lack of time. And loss of interest. Poems aren't delivered by mail, they're not on television, they rarely show up in the newspaper. After high school, after college, years go by before you — before we — ever read another poem. It doesn't even cross our minds to do such a thing.

But here's what I'm afraid of: that in eliminating poetry from our lives, we miss discovering a pursuit of pleasure that we didn't even know we needed.

The right poem can change how we see the world.

Several years ago, I came across Sharon Chmielarz's "New Water." She's not from North Carolina, didn't write this about North Carolina, but it doesn't matter. These words — the words of all poetry — transcend geographical boundaries. I've seen this scene played out before, with people I care about. I know you have, too.

All those years — almost a hundred —
the farm had hard water.
Hard orange. Buckets lined in orange.
Sink and tub and toilet, too,
once they got running water.
And now, in less than a lifetime,
just by changing the well's location,
in the same yard, mind you,
the water's soft, clear, delicious
   to drink.
All those years to shake your head over.

Look how sweet life has become;
you can see in the couple who live here,
their calmness as they sit at their table,
the beauty as they offer you new water
   to drink.

I love this poem. I keep it pinned at my desk, and I read it nearly every day. It reminds me to look for those small opportunities to make life better, the ones that may have been right in front of you, if you'd only noticed, if only you'd done something about it. "All those years to shake your head over. Look how sweet life has become."

That's what poetry can do. It reaches beyond our backyards, crosses our borders, and captures something elusive, those diamonds in the sky.

When we find the right verse, the one that makes us laugh, or cry, or sing out loud, we put those words in our pockets, and we carry them with us for the rest of our lives. *Os*

When Life Was So Tender

It was still summer until Labor Day, and then, magically, it was fall, even though the gauge on the thermometer said no way.

We wore our new fall clothes to school anyway. As soon as we got permission to put away our white patent leathers, we stood at the bus stop, sweating in wool wraparound skirts and ribbed kneesocks and brown Woolrich corduroys.

Our new outfits signaled a change, a transition to a new season, a time for reinvention.

So we parted our hair on a different side and flipped it up in wings and carried our new book bags stuffed with new filler paper, even though we still had reams spilling out from the top shelf of the chest of drawers in our bedrooms at home.

We wrote with fresh No. 2's because last year's were pockmarked with teeth prints and the erasers were worn down to nubs. We hooked fat Bic 4-Color ballpoints into the spiral of our clean-faced notebooks, and none of us could figure out why in the world black was one of the colors.

Everything was brand new. A time to start over. This was our chance to make a clean break from the year before, to try out a new style, to be someone in the eighth grade who we hadn't been in the seventh.

THREE MONTHS AGO — LAST SEASON — I moved. Sold my house and everything in it and bought a new house and all new furniture. A rolled-arm sofa in a pewter stripe; a tufted leather cocktail ottoman; a tight-backed reading chair and a lighted china cabinet and a desk made of honey-colored reclaimed wood. Everything brand new.

On the last week in my old house, I washed my car in the driveway.

It took me about an hour to finish, and before I wound the hose back onto its reel, I turned the nozzle toward my plants.

I soaked my impatiens and petunias, and drenched the basket filled with purple pansies hanging on a shepherd's hook next to the front door.

And then I saw them.

Five tiny baby birds, each one no bigger than my thumb, floating in the nest that had been scrabbled together in the middle of the basket. The birds were, at best, two days old. Their mouths gaped open; it looked like they were gasping.

Or screaming.

I didn't know what to do. Pick up the nest to drain the water? But wouldn't my human hand cause the mother to abandon her babies? Hadn't I read something about that once? What if I made things worse?

Horrified by the thought that I'd drowned these little creatures — I don't even kill spiders — I fled to the backyard and slumped down in the hammock. I buried my face in my hands and cried.

If I'd killed those baby birds, I couldn't bear it.

I stayed like this for a few hours, paralyzed by what I'd potentially inflicted. Eventually, I forced myself to face what I'd done.

I went back to the basket and saw the mother bird. She flew away when I got close, but then I saw those little baby birds in the nest, maws still gaping, but oh my gosh, thank God, thank God, they were alive. The water had drained. The birds were soaked, but they were hanging in there.

For the next few days, I watched these birds. They grew at an astonishing rate. By day three, I could see a trace of feathers. By day four, their eyes opened.

By day five, two birds had moved to the edge of the nest. They were moving their legs, inching forward. I'd never seen anything like this in my life. I was watching a transition. A transformation.

On day six, moving day, I taped an index card to the shepherd's hook: "Baby Birds. Do Not Disturb." I didn't want the new owners not to notice. And then I got in my car and drove away.

I'm heartbroken that I didn't get to see all the stages of the birds' development. I wish I'd seen them stand up. I wish I'd seen them preening, picking at their feathers, getting their new outfits ready. I wish I'd seen their wings begin to beat. I wish I'd seen the ruffling, the fluffing.

I wish I'd seen them leave the nest, taking their leaps into the great unknown, stretching their wings, and flying. *Os*

Full Service

My mother turns in to Steve's BP at Friendly Center in Greensboro, but instead of pulling in at the self-service pumps, where I normally go, she eases in beside the full-service station and waits.

Tommy, one of the service technicians, comes out. My mother rolls down her window and asks, in her earnest voice, "How you doing, honey?" and she means it.

She's got a headlight out, and she tells Tommy this, and he leans down toward the window to be eye level with my mother and says, "You do, huh? Well, bless your heart," and he means it, too.

He sets to pumping the gas, and she pulls the lever for the hood, and the mechanic disappears under there, and fiddles with some things, and then he comes out and says, "All right, Mrs. Hudson, got you fixed up. You're all set."

Tommy works at the station with his brother, Steve McKoin. Steve has owned this filling station for more than 20 years. He started working here in 1970, when he was 16 years old. When he finally bought the place in 1993, Steve's dad, Pops, came on to help. Pops died in 2012, and not a day goes by that Steve doesn't miss working with the man. Steve's wife, Cathy, works here, too, and Steve's two sons, Andy and Steve Jr., and Steve's nephew, Stacy. This place is important to the people who work here; they care about it. They learn from each other. They lean on each other.

WHEN I WAS 16, I WORKED IN MY MOM'S crafts shop. I wasn't the best employee — I was a teenager and distracted — but the shop was all we had, and we cared about it, too, the way Steve and his family do with their gas station. For years, I listened to my mother talk to customers who became friends.

Back then, I took for granted the, well, *familiarity* of family businesses. Most all the shops I knew were family-run, and I assumed all businesses, everywhere in the world, were this way and would be forever: Jimmy Southern's Scott's Bookstore, Harvey Ferree's Tank and Tummy gas stations, Carlton Cheek's One-Hour Martinizing dry cleaners. When my mom and I drove up to the door at Carlton's, he stopped what he was doing every time and came out to the car to greet us, palming a lemon or cherry lollipop for me.

There was Jim Shelton's Henry James Barbecue and Jim Maness's Golden Waffle, a wonderful local joint that no one would have mistaken for any other breakfast house.

There was Earlene Ward's Asheboro Ford and Eva Frye's dress shop. Eva called my mother whenever she got new clothing in, and she was quick to tell you to take something off if it just didn't look good. I remember the labels inside the neckbands at Eva's: her name, embroidered in gold thread. We bought our carpet and wallpaper from Ken and Sally Cornwell's Interiors/Exteriors. My mother's first cash register for her shop came from Connell Philips's Business Supply, and I bought my first typewriter, an IBM Selectric III with lift-off correction tape, from there, too. I still remember loading that 30-pound steel machine into my car to take to college. It never occurred to me that, one day, something new would come along to take its place.

If you lived in Asheboro, you knew all these businesses by heart. If you didn't, I guarantee you had similar ones in your town, too. And I hope that when you walked in, somebody — a clerk or a mechanic or a waitress or a salesperson or a bank teller — knew your name. Asked you how you were. We didn't call this customer service. Instead, it was, simply, kindness.

I hope nothing ever comes along to take the place of that. *OS*

40

Animal Rescue

A lifelong friendship,
covered in fur.

The little black dog wore a yellow bandanna patterned with tiny monkeys — Curious George — around her neck. She sat on the curb in the parking lot of a shopping center, one of about a dozen animals in a pet adoption fair, but she was off to the side, away from the other dogs, all by herself.

She thumped her tail and lifted her head expectantly whenever someone walked by. Everyone beelined toward the yellow Labs, the golden retrievers.

Nobody stopped to pet the little black dog.

She was 5 months old, a border collie mutt. She'd been at the shelter nearly all her life, picked up as an abandoned, weeks-old stray, a sweet little dog that nobody wanted.

I loved her immediately.

I scooped her up and signed some papers and paid the adoption fee — as it turned out, she was half off; I didn't know this until later, but her time at the shelter had expired. She was slated for euthanasia the next week.

Instead, she came home to live with me. I named her Wilma.

A FEW DAYS INTO OUR NEW RELATIONship, Wilma started circling my legs, nipping at my ankles, barking at me. I tried to fend off her bites, and I broke down crying because I thought I'd brought home an aggressive dog, and what would happen now?

I took her to the vet, who explained this about the breed: Wilma is a herding dog. She was herding me.

She's bred for work, the vet said. She needs a job. She needs a purpose.

So Wilma and I started walking.

We walked a mile in the morning before I went to work.

At lunch, we walked another mile. After work, another mile.

We made a route for ourselves, a

routine, and I saw the relief settle into her body.

I felt it in mine, too.

Can we call an animal a companion? A friend?

I think so. Our kinship with animals develops early on. Some of our first toys are stuffed animals. We pat the bunny. We bring home a goldfish from the fair. We climb into bed with a bear tucked under our arm, a silent confidant to whisper our dreams to. We fall in love with Wilbur the pig. With Frog and Toad. With Curious George. We talk to our cats and our dogs and our horses and our chickens, and, although they never talk back, we're grateful they listen.

I am sure of this: Animals teach us how to be better humans.

If it's possible to call an animal a companion — a friend — then I've done that. Wilma has been by my side now for 13 years. She's seen sickness and sadness and fear and excitement and happiness and hope — all the emotions that make a life. Through it all, her response is the same: She lifts her head. She thumps her tail on the floor. Maybe she thinks it's her job, her purpose. I don't know. But every time, it helps.

WILMA'S SLOWED DOWN SOME NOW. Some days, we get a few steps out the front door, and she stops, then turns back toward the house, head down, tail tucked. I've learned that some days aren't so good for walking.

On those days, we sit outside. She finds a spot in the sunshine — I think the warmth feels good on her back — and we listen to the birds and the neighborhood kids playing basketball and the lawnmowers in the distance, and we take in the faint smell of cut grass and wild onions lifted up by the breeze. Wilma dozes. Her hind legs kick as if she's running, and I can't help but smile and think, "Go, dog, go."

I hope that whatever you're running toward, it's a mighty good place. *Os*

Easy Listening

It was a stereo, not a radio, even though the box said it came from Radio Shack. And it was a birthday present, maybe even the best one I ever got, the one that crossed me over from the era of the 1970s into the 1980s, formative years, when I traded glasses for contact lenses and swabbed Sea Breeze on my face at night.

My new stereo was sleek and modern and beautiful. Silver and chrome, the front of it flush with not one, but two cassette tape decks, in case I wanted to *dub* something, whatever that meant.

Wires ran out the back of the stereo and connected to two three-foot-tall speakers, each one encased in a brown walnut veneer. Those speakers took up as much floor space as a small sofa, and I had to rearrange the furniture in my bedroom to make everything fit.

The stereo marked my move away from the scratchy records that I spent my childhood playing on a portable turntable. When I got the new system set up, I shoved the old record player, with its flimsy plastic dustcover, to the back of my bedroom closet, along with an aging stack of albums, including John Denver's *Back Home Again*, from which I had played "Annie's Song" over and over, and Glen Campbell's *Rhinestone Cowboy*.

MY NEW STEREO CALLED FOR A DIFFERent kind of music, something that sounded the way the thing looked: sleek and modern and silver and chrome.

I looked for new music, and I found it — on Casey Kasem's "American Top 40" countdown on Friday nights; in the bins at Disc Jockey, a record store in the mall; in the back pages of my grandmother's *Good Housekeeping* magazines, advertisements for cassettes sent straight to your house from the Columbia Record Club. I taped a penny to the postcard and sent off for 12 cassettes.

At night, I sequestered myself in my room — an act of freedom rather than punishment — and spent hours plopped in a beanbag chair, listening to music, my music, new music, rewinding cassette tapes, writing down lyrics in a notebook so I could memorize them. The Human League and Soft Cell and Queen and Dexys Midnight Runners and New Order, mostly electronic, synthesized sounds that were a sharp contrast from The Everly Brothers that played on my dad's small radio in the garage, the one with the antenna that flopped if it wasn't leaning against the radio's handle, and from the Conway Twitty and Crystal Gayle songs my mother hummed when she folded laundry.

At school, in the lunchroom, on the bus, everyone I knew talked about music. Boys carved band logos into the backs of the chairs in front of them; we wore T-shirts advertising a place called the Hard Rock Cafe that was in cities none of us had ever been to. We made mixtapes, spending hours arranging the order of songs — this was why my stereo had dual cassettes! — for each other. I didn't know it then, but we were creating a common soundtrack of belonging, and though our English teachers encouraged us to follow the beat of a different drummer, I have to wonder: Were we doing that at all? Did we even want to?

Music gave us identity. What we listened to told us who we were. And we needed that.

Over the years, my taste moved from New Wave to pop to grunge to bluegrass to blues and jazz and classical. I like it all, and I suppose that's the point of music, too, right? To build on what came before. And then to expand, to reach, to stretch. To seek out those sweet, new sounds, the ones that fill our ears and our hearts and our horizons, the songs that give meaning to who we'll become next. *Os*

a Wish *for* Christmas

Twelve children. A whole dozen, can you even imagine? Eight girls and four boys, and they all lived with their mama and daddy in a farmhouse with no electricity, no running water, in Guilford County.

Clifton. Ralph. Clyde. Grant (who, oddly, they all called Pete). Cora. Irene. Lucille. Mamie. Pearl. Ruth. Nancy. And Dorothy.

Dorothy is my grandmother, my mama's mama. Dorothy Dean Newman Coble Wright. But all my life, she's been Grandma Dot to me.

On December 1, Grandma Dot turns 86 years old. Can you even imagine all the changes she's seen in her long life, from the time she was a little girl living on that farm?

Her daddy, my great-grandfather, raised tobacco and watermelons and everything they put on the table for supper. Everyone, all those 12 children, helped in the fields. At night, the kids took their baths in a big tub; everyone got in the same water, one right after the other. Grandma Dot's mama heated the water on the woodstove and poured it in, refilling the bath after each child got out, to keep it warm.

In the mornings, the girls dressed in sacks that had once been filled with feed for the cows and pigs. In the fall, all the children got a new pair of shoes for school. Nights after supper, when it got dark, they played Chinese checkers, which was better than regular checkers because six kids could play at a time.

They didn't have many toys. The boys played hide-and-seek outside. The girls made their dolls out of rags and corn husks. They painted the shucks. They plaited the silks for hair.

Christmas, such an anticipatory time for children now, wasn't a big deal in the 1920s and '30s, at least not for farm kids in North Carolina whose family didn't have any money.

On Christmas Eve, Grandma Dot's daddy cut a cedar from the woods behind the house and dragged it inside. All the children sat together by the tree, breathing in the clean and camphorous smell until it was time to go to bed. There were no stockings hanging by the fireplace, but on Christmas morning, the children woke to find 12 paper bags under the tree. Each bag was carefully folded over. Each bag had a child's name scrawled in pencil on the front. Each bag held a box of raisins, an apple, an orange, a smattering of pecans.

Those children had never been happier than when they got that fruit. Can you even imagine? And they spun around right there in the room, holding their bags and chanting happily, "Santy Claus done come, Santy Claus done come!" Like it was a miracle.

AT AGE 19, GRANDMA DOT GOT MARried. She and her husband-to-be, my grandfather, went to the preacher's house, the two of them said "I do," and when they came out of the parsonage, her sisters were standing outside throwing rice, and everyone whooped and hollered and spun around right there on the porch, and then Grandma Dot, who wasn't a grandma yet at all, just Dorothy Dean Newman Coble, saw something else mixed in with all that rice flying around: snow. It was snowing to beat the band. Can you even imagine? And just then she realized it was Christmas Eve. How about that: These two young kids had just gotten married on December 24, 1948, my grandmother with her whole life stretched out in front of her, yet to be opened, full of hope and happiness and, yes, heartbreak, too, for these are all the things that make a long life, aren't they? And isn't that what we all wish for — for ourselves and everyone we love, and not just at Christmastime but always and every day — to find ourselves spinning and twirling in tossed rice and falling snow, clutching paper bags full of sweet oranges for as long as possible? Can you even imagine? *OS*

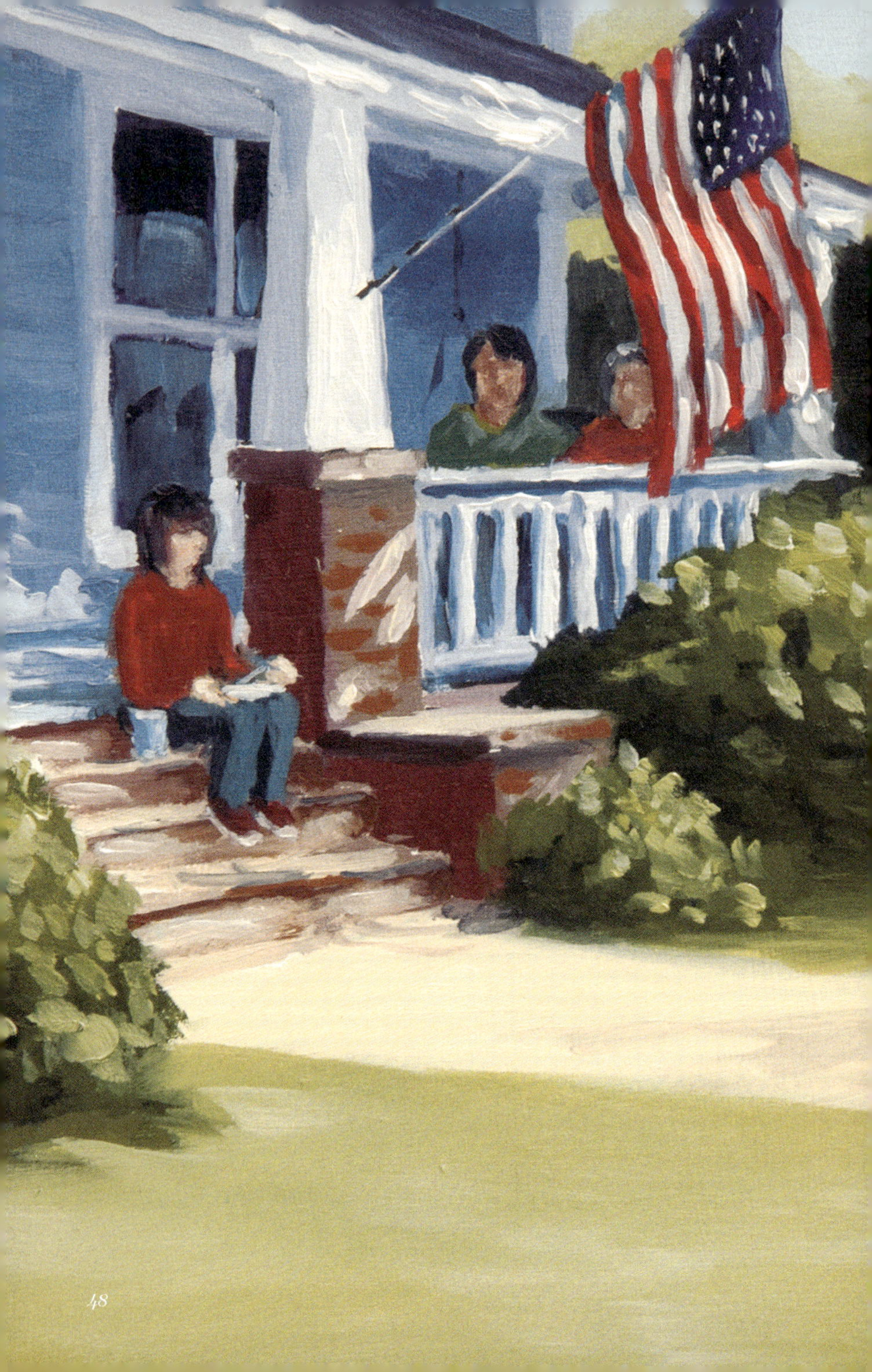

Midsummer Classic

It's what's in the middle that matters.

Here is July 1: the 182nd day of the year, the halfway point, the midsection of 2014, with 183 days left.

By now, we're halfway to Christmas, halfway to winter, halfway to new resolutions. We mark our halfway points by looking toward the end.

I'm 45 years old, and if statistics hold, I'm just past the midpoint of my life. A few years ago, someone told me that it isn't the dates on either end of a tombstone that matters, but, rather, the dash in the middle. I like that. The stuff in the middle — the filler — is what makes us.

The middle is the peak of the mountain. It's the arc in the basketball free throw. It's the cream in the Oreo cookie. It's the bridge in the Beach Boys' "Wouldn't It Be Nice." It's second base on a baseball field. It's the line up a tree where the trunk stops and the peaches hang. It's the sweet spot at the top of the roller coaster, the pivot where the car balances for that split second before the laws of physics engage and the rider — that's you, that's me — changes direction.

The midpoint marks the contrast between everything that came before and everything that comes after, but sometimes we get so focused on how things will turn out — or we get bogged down worrying about the past — that we forget to live in our middle moments, the ones that seem insignificant because they don't come with the fanfare of beginnings or endings.

But some middle moments stay with us.

HERE IS JULY 4, MANY YEARS AGO: MY grandmother unspools the flag and hangs it from the pole off the porch.

By noon, here comes the family: aunts, uncles, cousins — Abe and Jade and Stevra and Pete and Kent and Jimmy — and my mom and dad, who closed their shop for the holiday.

My grandfather goes out for a bag of ice and then pulls the Proctor Silex ice cream churn from the basement, the one with the wood-paneled sides and an electric motor that sits on top.

We all eat cold fried chicken from paper plates on the porch, and my grandmother pours a mixture — egg yolks and milk and vanilla and sugar — into the metal can and sets it in the bucket and layers in ice and rock salt.

She pops the brown power unit on top, and the can hums as it turns around and around the dasher, and the ice melts and runs out the holes in the bucket's side, and my grandfather fetches towels to wrap around the base to keep the salty-cold water from spilling onto the porch, and we all sit and dangle our legs from the swing and watch bees flit in and out of the rose bushes, and it is the greatest day.

And I remember this, too: the flag flapping against a startlingly blue sky and the smell of sweet shrub in the air and a sense that the world is as full and ripe as it will ever get — a season in full swing, the midpoint of summer, no hint of the past, no thought to the future.

Surely, the moment — this moment — will last forever.

Just then someone yells "Hill!" and my cousins and I run to the hill past the house and scamper to the top and lie down with our arms tucked into our chests and hurl ourselves down that hill, rolling, rolling, rolling, and I don't remember now the top or the end, just the middle, just the spot where we pick up momentum and there is absolutely no stopping, not even if we wanted to. *Os*

Beauty *is in the* Eye

When I was in the fourth grade, a nurse came into our classroom at Farmer School and taped an eye chart full of letter E's to the chalkboard. One at a time, each student got up from his desk, stood behind the piece of yellow tape the nurse had stuck to the floor, held a piece of cardboard to cover one eye, and stared straight ahead at the chart, turning his hand up, down, right, or left, depending on which way the tines of the E pointed.

When it was my turn, I stood behind the yellow tape. I looked toward the chalkboard. But I didn't see any E's, not even the biggest one at the top of the chart.

I couldn't even see the chart.

The nurse whispered to the teacher.

I went home with a note telling my parents to take me to a doctor immediately. In a few days, I slid on my first pair of glasses, ugly brown plastic frames that made me look bookish and nerdy in the way no elementary school student wants to look.

BUT STILL. I WAS LUCKY. MY SCHOOL recognized pretty early on that I had vision problems — but it wasn't that way when my mother was in school.

Back then, nobody noticed how close she sat to the chalkboard. No one noticed how she leaned in to her schoolbooks, to try to see the print. No one noticed how she squinted when she tried to read.

Why didn't you go to a doctor, Mama? She shrugs. Just wasn't something anyone did. Not children, anyway. Her teacher didn't know she was having trouble seeing. Her parents didn't, either. Nobody talked about it.

She got her first pair of glasses when she was 16 years old; as it turned out, she couldn't pass the driver's test and wasn't allowed to get her license without glasses. So for the first time, she went to a doctor. He told her she'd be blind by age 35.

Thankfully, that didn't happen, but I don't remember ever seeing my mother without her glasses. They're just a part of her face, the same way I recognize the beauty mark near her mouth, and to me, those glasses are mostly invisible anyway. When I look at her, I see past the glasses to her green eyes instead, the beautiful ones that light up when my dad smiles at her. The ones that sparkle when she laughs. The ones that shine when she hugs me.

A few months ago, my mother was diagnosed with macular degeneration. The doctor changed her glasses prescription; the lenses are thick, and she's adjusting. He gave her some pills to take. He told her that he'd monitor her condition.

She doesn't talk about it, but I know she's worried.

My mother looks at everything now as if she's seeing it for the first time. She drinks her coffee by the kitchen window in the morning and watches for the yellow finches to come. She notices the moon rising at night. She looks — really looks — at her little brother's face when he visits, and at her friend Linda when they go out for a sandwich at Subway. She watches my dad when he nods off to sleep in his chair. It's as if she's memorizing every detail, locking these images into some kind of brain vault, visions she can retrieve when she closes her eyes.

It won't matter how thick her glasses get, or how much her vision deteriorates. My mother sees with her heart. And I don't know of a more beautiful sight than that. *Os*

From *the* Booth

In the winter, moisture condenses on the front windows, because it's cold out there and it's warm in here, in this place where steam rises from the grill, and rye bread and onion rolls sizzle in butter, and cheeses melt and seep out the sides of sandwiches named Rachel and Arlington and Italian Sailor.

A metal floor stand reads "Please Seat Yourself," but the place is packed — it's always packed — and the booths are filled. Given a choice, I'll always take a booth; who wouldn't? So comforting and cave-like, an interior room within a room, a subconscious reminder of the way we tented the den with quilts or climbed into packing boxes when we were children, gravitating toward an inherent need to be contained. To be held in.

So I wait next to the glass case stocked with bagels.

Of course this place has bagels — the deli's name is Lox, Stock & Bagel, after all — and it has meat and cheese, too, piles of it in another glass case, pastrami and prosciutto and kosher bologna, and Colby and Muenster and mozzarella, all of it listed on a board with by-the-pound prices.

A seat opens, and I scoot into a hard-backed wooden booth, brown-paneled, just like the walls. Everything is brown here. Even the tabletops are a deep red-brown, and brown is good. Brown is warm.

A couple of menus, single laminated sheets, sit on top of the napkin dispenser, but in all my years of coming here, I've never looked at a menu.

A waitress brings me water in a plastic cup and asks what'll I have.

I say a Reuben. Given a choice, I'll always take a Reuben, that perfect marriage of stacked corned beef and melted Swiss and sauerkraut and Russian dressing. It was the first sandwich I ever ate in a restaurant, a grown-up choice I made at my dad's sandwich shop when I was 10 years old.

A few minutes later, the waitress sets down a brown plastic basket — no plate — my sandwich tucked inside on plain waxed paper. A handful of chips in the basket. A dill pickle spear.

I eat slowly, and then somehow it's 30 years ago as much as it's today, and I hold that sandwich and think about so much.

An older lady sits at a table beside me. She's by herself, like I am, and her cane, which has been propped on the chair beside her, falls to the floor.

I get up, pick up her cane, position it a little closer to her. "That thing just won't stay put," she says, shaking her head, smiling at me. Her thin hands hold a plastic fork, and she dabs at a small Styrofoam bowl of baked beans. Her basket holds half of an egg salad sandwich.

She's here for supper, like I am, and I wonder if she has, at home in her cabinet like I do, a can of Underwood Deviled Ham with its white paper label and the red devil with the pitchfork. I wonder if she has tuna fish packed in oil, like I do. I wonder if she has a tub of pimento cheese, Ruth's, or a container of chicken salad, fixings for emergency sandwiches for the days when she doesn't drive here, for the days when it's raining or there's a chance of sleet or, for whatever reason, she just doesn't feel like getting out.

But that's not this day, thankfully, and so the two of us sit, wordlessly enjoying our meals. Given a choice, I — and maybe this lady, too — will always look for a place like this one, where the atmosphere is warm and strangers are kind, and the food isn't meant to be complicated or cut with a knife and fork, but simply picked up and held. *OS*

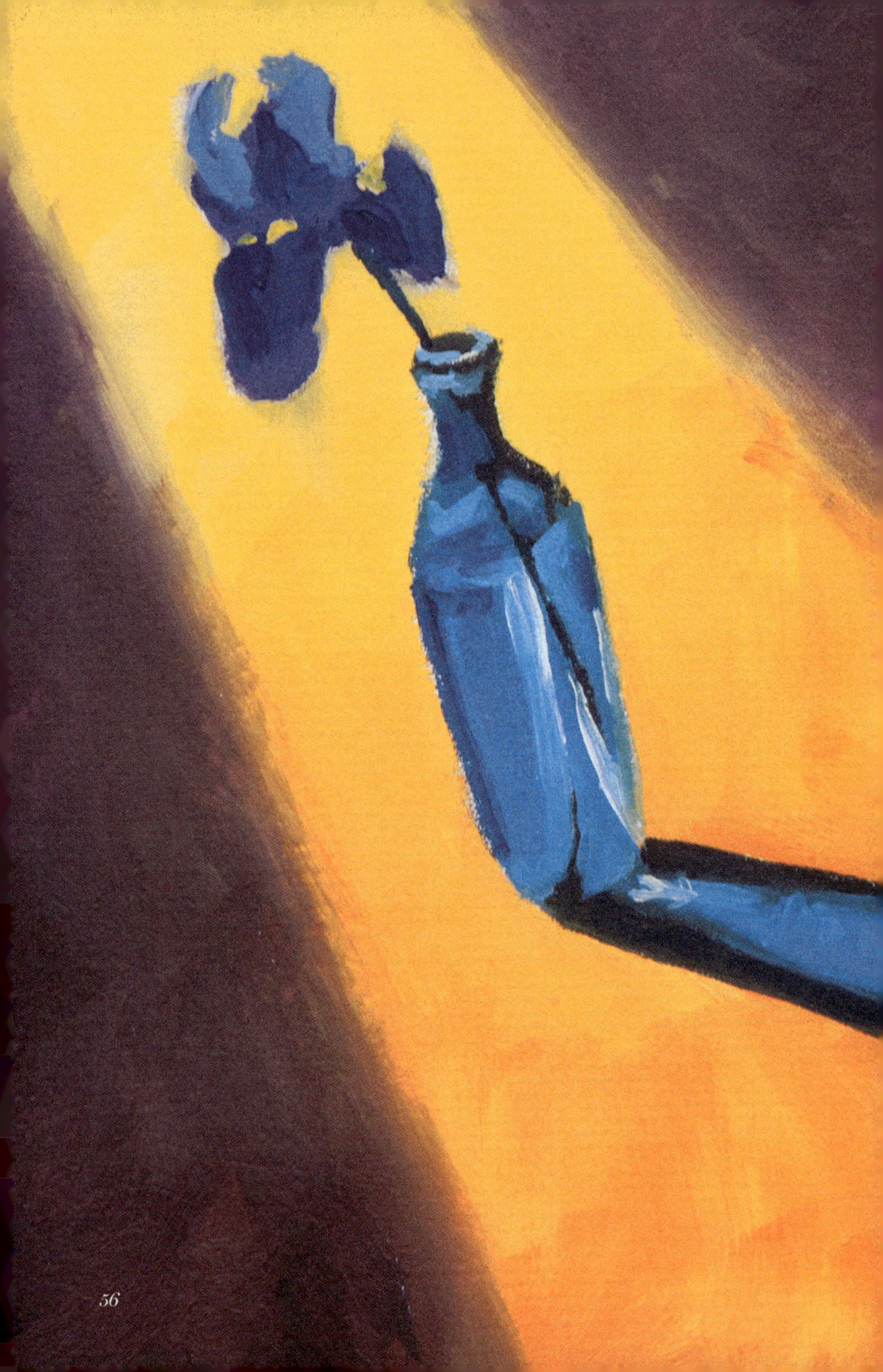

the Language of Flowers

Filling a house — and a heart — with blooms from the backyard.

Orchids were everywhere at The Fresh Market, so that's what I got for my side table. And after our bitter winter, the tulips looked fresh and bright, so I got a bunch of those, too, and made a pretty arrangement in a water glass for my kitchen table. And I couldn't leave the store without those stems of stargazer lilies and a cluster of Lenten roses that have now found a place on the nightstand beside my bed.

I've taken to filling my house with fresh flowers every week, and even I am surprised at how transformative these blooms are, how they effortlessly change the personality of a space.

Until recently, I never spoke the language of flowers. Or rather, flowers never spoke to me, not the way they have to so many people I know, and certainly not the way they spoke to my grandmother.

SHE HAD A PERENNIAL GARDEN IN HER backyard — perennials because she didn't have much money to replant flowers every year — and I can see her standing out there now, the sleeves of her white cotton blouse rolled to the elbows, a cigarette held between two fingers, the sun catching the tiny rhinestones in the upsweep of her cat-eye frames. She was the epitome of Southern grace in that garden, and it seemed the flowers she grew stood upright just for her.

She weeded and watered and tended and dug in the dirt and, in the spring, she got her reward when the garden exploded in abundance, more color and scent than any yard could possibly contain, and off she went with the shears on Saturday mornings, carting armfuls of cuttings into the house and spreading the flowers across the kitchen table. She set to stripping leaves and snipping stems on the diagonal, and I, transfixed by television cartoons, was ignorant of whatever she was doing.

I wish I'd paid more attention.

Because then I would've noticed how she arranged the tall branches of brilliant yellow forsythia in cut-crystal trumpet vases, fanning the woody stalks into a spray that looked like rays of sunshine.

I would've watched how she tucked blueberry-hued hyacinths, no longer than her hand, into squat, knobby milk glass.

I would've seen how she trained her American Beauty roses to climb the trellis behind the porch swing. I would've helped her water the hydrangeas and bury pennies in the dirt to turn them blue — because blue is the prettiest color against white clapboard. I would've carried the tin can full of day-old Maxwell House coffee grounds to the edge of the garden and sprinkled the contents around the base of the camellia bush.

I would've laughed more when she plucked yellow buttercups and waved them under my chin until I admitted to liking butter — "I do like it, Grandma, I do!" — and I would've let her tickle me until I dissolved into a fit of giggles, and I would've put my hand on her back to steady her when she stretched to reach the high branches from the magnolia tree, and I would've filled the ceramic dishes with water for floating those magnolia blooms, one in every room.

I would've breathed in deeper that fragrance, like the sweetest syrup, and held it inside for as long as possible.

And I would've gone out to the garden for my grandmother when she was no longer able to and picked a bouquet of her favorites: irises, the violet and blue and magenta and yellow ones. The ones named for Iris in Greek mythology, the goddess of the rainbow, the link between sea and sky, the one who carries all the messages between heaven and earth. *Os*

in Search *of* Safe Places

My evening walk takes me past Fire Station #43 on Lake Jeanette Road in Greensboro. An American flag and a black-and-red Fire Department flag fly from a pole in front of the brick building. You know what's inside this building, of course, but maybe you've never noticed the small sign on the outside, the yellow, diamond-shaped emblem, mounted on the brick. The sign proclaims this spot as a Safe Place.

I know this symbol is a national designation for children in difficult situations, a shelter for youth in trouble, and yet when I see the sign, it makes me think this: We all need our safe places.

YEARS AGO, I WENT TO CHURCH EVERY Sunday with my grandmother. We snugged into the same pew every week

— she on the inside and me on the aisle — and midway through the hour, just when I started to get squirmy, she reached into her purse and palmed something into my hand, a Brach's Star Brite peppermint or a Luden's Wild Cherry cough drop. Just like that, my shoulders dropped, and I was still.

After church, we ate lunch at the Apple House Cafeteria in the Randolph Mall in Asheboro. We pushed our plastic cafeteria trays forward on the metal rail, and those trays held the same things every time: a small bowl of carrot salad and a vegetable plate for her, baked spaghetti for me. I didn't think so much about why we got the same thing every time, but now I know why. There was comfort in the familiar.

We snugged into our regular booth — me close to the wall and she on the aisle — and there were always streams of people who came by to say hello, to reach for my grandmother's hand, to ask how she was doing, to promise that they were coming by soon to see her flower garden or to have a slice of pound cake. We stayed in the restaurant for hours, long after we'd eaten, and now I know why. There was comfort in people.

On the days when I wasn't with my grandmother, I read my books, and I played in the woods behind my house. Sat on high rocks, which became thrones, and scrambled over logs, which became the backs of dinosaurs. Made leaf boats and floated them downstream in the creek, and I was utterly happy, and now I know why. There was comfort in solitude, too.

And maybe I wasn't the only creature to realize such a thing. I was in those woods the first time I saw a deer up close. It was a mighty, antlered thing, so big, and I was so small, but both of us were surprised, each of us startled to come upon the other. We froze. I stood still. The deer stood still. We were sending a mutual message: "Don't worry, I won't hurt you."

Eventually the deer turned and bounded back the way he'd come, retreating deeper into his own safe place. I watched for as long as I could, until he simply blended into the forest and vanished.

I wish for places like this now — a small church, a cozy restaurant booth, the deep of the woods. When you're young, it seems these places are easier to come by. Maybe what I'm wishing for isn't a physical place at all, but something we all want — a living connection of compassion. A steady hand on a shoulder. A sign to let us know that everything is all right. *OS*

One Day *in* May

May 7 is my mother's birthday, a milestone birthday, and the other day, while we were sitting outside Baskin-Robbins eating ice-cream cones, she said out loud, *What have I been doing all these years?*

Now that's a question.

She was leaning back in the chair, kicking her crossed leg, letting the sun warm her face, and she was twirling that ice cream cone like mad in her hand, like she was winding a watch.

I could see that she was happy. Content. But her question hung in the air.

"What have I been doing all these years?"

Like she'd wasted them. Or misused them. Or wished she'd done something differently.

Oh, Mama.

If you don't mind, may I remind you? You went from being a little girl who I never knew, who got so excited over her first — and only — birthday cake that your own mother ordered with a doll in the middle, the doll's dress fanning out in thick frosting, to a high school senior with a teased beehive and a blue satin prom gown. You kept your mouth closed when you smiled, and I know it's because you thought your teeth weren't nice enough, but then one day you realized that goodness, that kindness, have nothing to do with teeth. You got a beautician's license to do hair, but then you met my dad, so handsome and hearty, and you got married instead. And then you had me. And I hope you see how I look at you and wonder how I will ever endure this earth without you, although I recognize that one day I will have to, and I don't like thinking about that at all, but we're being honest here, and so there it is.

If you don't mind, may I remind you that you started a thriving small business when you were only 22 years old, and even now I get calls from so many people, readers of this magazine who remember your crafts store in Asheboro with such fondness. They remember how well you treated them when they brought in their cross-stitched samplers and crocheted sweaters and tole-painted footstools for you to admire, and they tell me about your genuine laugh and your infectious enthusiasm — and I see it, every day, not only in you, but, somehow, now it's jumped to me, too, because, oh, Mama, this is what you've been doing all these years: saturating the spirit of everyone around you with joy.

If you don't mind, may I remind you that when you closed your store after a long, 20-year run, you got your first job, selling furniture, and you were so good at it, the way you are so good at everything you do. At making silky meringue for the tops of your lemon and chocolate pies; at turning down a bed and smoothing the sheets so they seem cool when someone has a temperature; at lining a front walkway with marigolds, so sunny and cheerful; at stopping in to see a friend who's having a hard time; at pushing a broom across a floor to make everything so clean and fresh.

How we spend our days is, of course, how we spend our lives, says the writer Annie Dillard, and isn't that the truth? Isn't that just exactly right?

What have you been doing all these years? You've been making every day better for the people who love you, just by being alive in this world.

Happy birthday, Mama. And Mother's Day, too.

What a gift. *OS*

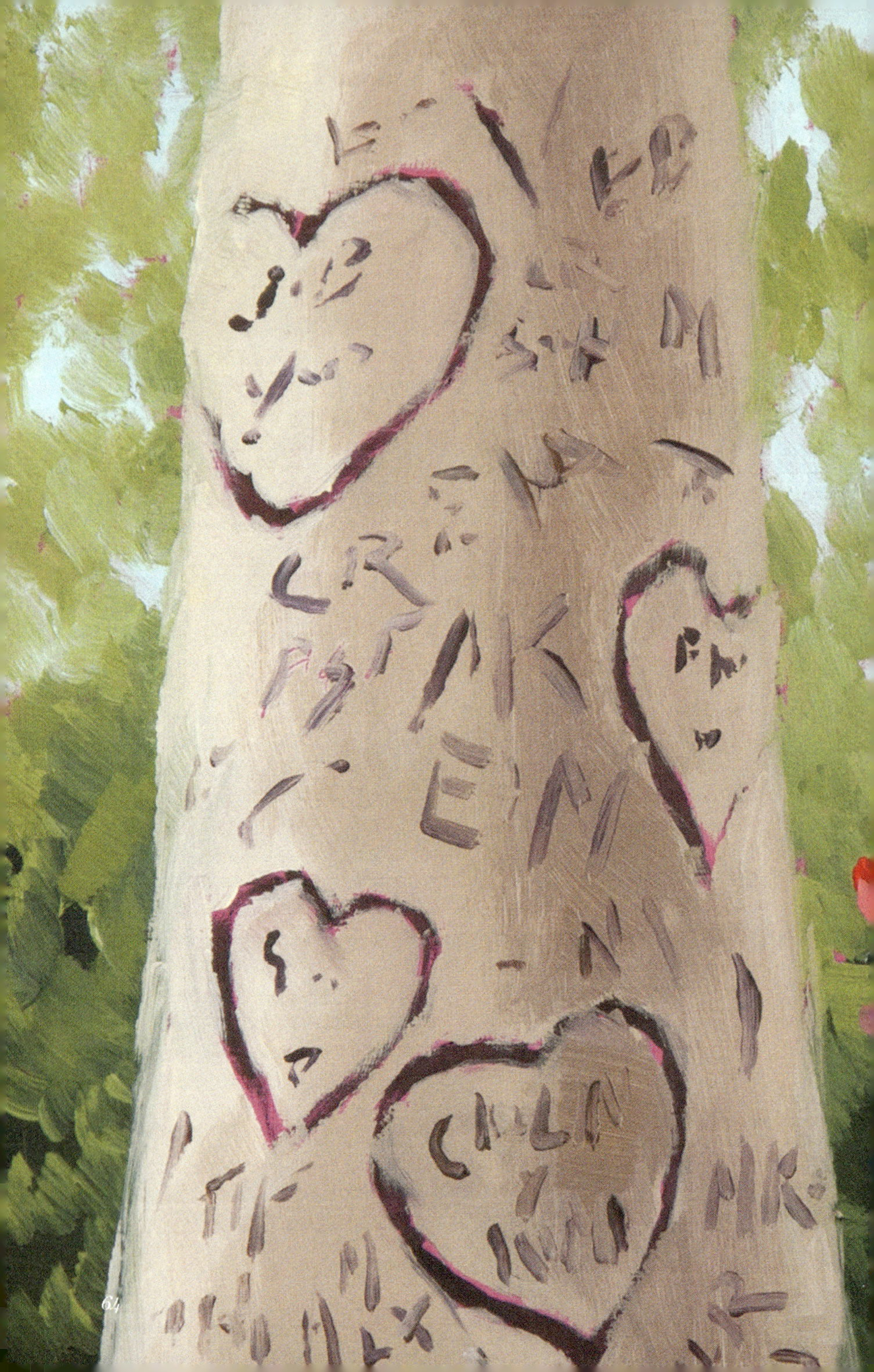

Leaving a Mark

Finding ways to leave a legacy.

We were walking downtown, my grandmother and I, to watch an artist paint a mural on the side of the Ross building in Asheboro. It was 1976, a bicentennial year, a year of commemoration. I was 6 years old.

We held hands, and every so often, my grandmother swung her arm, lifting me slightly off the ground. I squealed and we kept walking, her sterling-silver charm bracelet tinkling against our wrists.

Maybe because I was eye level with it, I remember everything about that bracelet. How it draped across the small bone at the base of her hand. How she kept it polished, wiping each charm with Wright's Silver Cream. A dozen charms dangled from the bracelet, each one in the shape of a silhouetted head, each one engraved with a name, not just grandchildren, but all her family, all of us, everyone she cared about.

My name was on one of those charms: "Elizabeth Ann," written in tiny, delicate script. I found it soothing to trace my fingers across those charms, not grasping, of course, the significance of so many names permanently etched, something that would, one day, be evidence that we were here, that we existed, that we were loved.

> We all hope for permanence, don't we? And we do what we can to make it so.

That bracelet belongs to me now. It's too small for my wrist, but when I hold it, the charms still clink together, and I remember.

I thought about this the other day when I was walking in Greensboro's Tanger Family Bicentennial Garden, the memory triggered because the park was created in 1976, a bicentennial year, a year of commemoration, or maybe it

66 LEAVING A MARK

was because we were working on an issue devoted to love and anniversaries.

I was lost in thought — oh, for someone to reach down and swing my arm, lift me off my feet, just for one moment — and then I passed by one of my favorite spots, a small grove behind the azalea and camellia bushes. Here, there's a towering American beech, completely covered in carvings.

I sat down at the base of the tree and started reading, tracing my fingers across the smooth, silvery bark, trying to make out the letters, the dates, the names.

So many names.

Must be 100 or more cut into this tree. Tracey and Jay. Mark and Trish. Megan and Russell. Angela and Sean.

Lucy. Anna. Ed.

E.B. + S.K. BW and MC. W+K.

Five hearts, maybe more, carved into the bark. In one place, the carving reads, "I am sorry."

I wonder about that one.

Beech trees can live up to 300 years, and I think about how long this one has been wearing all these names, how long these etchings have been in place, proof that someone was here. That someone existed. That someone was loved.

We all hope for permanence, don't we? And we do what we can to make it so, leaving our messages in places where others might see them.

I see these messages all over this state, declarations of love, of affection, even of apology. They're carved on trees in Greensboro's parks, on Asheville's trails, in Southern Pines' woods. They're scratched into the sand with a stick at Emerald Isle, at Ocean Isle. They're painted on the sides of boats in Beaufort, in Oriental, in Swan Quarter. I see wooden benches with bronze plaques mounted to their backs and commemorative bricks set in pathways in Fayetteville, in Jacksonville, in Salisbury. And everywhere, I see fields of stone markers — smooth, silvery granite — names and dates and etchings of affections, each one a permanent memorial, but also something more, a message to all of us that someone was here. That someone existed. That someone was loved. *OS*

One *of* Us

First, it was a job.
    Thirteen people in an office, and I became the 14th person hired.

On my first day, I was given a desk and a telephone. We didn't have the Internet. We weren't using email. There was no website. We had a coffeemaker, but no sink. We refilled the pot with water from the bathroom.

The magazine was small then. There were stories to edit, but not many. There were ads to sell, but not many. The magazine topped out at 48 pages. Maybe you remember it.

We had 28,000 readers.

Maybe you were one of them.

Oh, we all wanted this magazine to be so good, the best thing you'd ever seen. We spent our days trying to build something special, to create something you'd be proud to welcome into your home. We worked hard. It was a job first.

But then look what happened.

One of us, we found out, had a new grandchild. We pooled our money and bought a silver frame. One of us got engaged. We made layer cakes and wrote toasts. All of us had birthdays. We ate lunches together. We threw parties for each other.

We arranged potlucks in our break room. One of us plugged in a Crock-Pot and made chili. One of us plugged in a Crock-Pot and made barbecue. One of us made a run to Reidsville to pick up a gallon of Short Sugar's barbecue sauce.

When the magazine grew and the staff expanded and we moved to a bigger building, one of us set up tables in the hallway and all of us piled food on those, plates of deviled eggs and seven-layer salads. For Hanukkah, one of us put on an apron, hauled in 20 pounds of potatoes, grated each one by hand, and fried latkes in four skillets.

All of us have collectively gained and lost hundreds of pounds.

When my dad spent nearly a month in the hospital, one of us filled a cooler with dinners for my mother and me.

I couldn't believe it.

What's a family without food?

For Christmas, all of us decorated a tree and filled our conference room with gifts for the Children's Home Society of North Carolina, for kids who otherwise wouldn't get any presents on Christmas morning. One year, after a terrible storm, one of us lost our house to a fallen tree. The loss made all of us sick.

What's a family without empathy?

We've gone to funerals.

At first, I never went to funerals, thinking I'd be uncomfortable or unwelcome among people who weren't my family.

I know better now. We are no longer afraid or embarrassed to cry in front of each other.

What's a family without support?

THERE ARE MORE OF US NOW — 48 PEO-ple work here. And there are more of you, too, moving steadily toward 200,000 subscribers to this magazine. We have the Internet and email and a website. It's all hard for me to believe, how fast all these years have gone by.

First, it was a job. But then it became something else, and now, look what's happened. Together, we've watched Cedar Island fishermen set their pound nets and we've saluted our veterans at Fort Bragg, Camp Lejeune, Seymour Johnson. We've climbed every lighthouse and caught lightning bugs in Mason jars and crossed the swinging bridge at Grandfather Mountain. We've listened to Doc and Earl and the Avetts. We've eaten pork chop sandwiches in Mount Airy and pancakes in Maggie Valley and mounds of barbecue from Lexington to Wilson. We've driven Highway 64 and I-40 and 421, and you've been right there with us, every month. You're one of us, too.

What's family without each other? This year marks my 19th anniversary at *Our State*. Thank you for being a part of my life. Thank you for allowing us to be a part of yours.

I hope you don't mind if I feel like celebrating. ***OS***

Peace *in the* Valley

And then, after the open worship — it's a Quaker church; congregants speak aloud when moved by the spirit — and the singing of "Simple Gifts," led by Joe Gamble, former teacher at Trinity High School for whom the Joseph P. Gamble Center for Performing Arts is now named, a guitarist moved to the front, got settled, strummed a C chord, and started singing, low and slow:

"Well, I'm tired and so weary
But I must go along
Till the Lord comes and calls me,
Calls me away ..."

You'd think it'd be easy to sit in a church pew and listen to a rendition of "Peace in the Valley," one of the most beautiful songs ever written, but you'd be wrong.

If you weren't looking around, if you were focused instead on the church bulletin or the way the sanctuary was drawing in slants of sunlight, you'd miss the hung head of my uncle — the other one, the living one, the one who took off his Korean War Veteran cap before he walked into this church — and you'd miss the slumped shoulders of my two cousins sitting in the front pew, tall, strong men who just lost their dad and today seem just a little bit smaller. You'd miss the absence of my dad, whose health wouldn't let him attend the service for his older brother, and you'd miss seeing how my mother, sitting beside me, clenched a tissue, and how we all fought back tears until we didn't.

THE BABY UP FRONT — SHE BELONGS TO one of those cousins with the slumped shoulders — is crying or laughing or cooing (babies just don't know how to do memorial services, do they?) but the noise is sweet and happy and it sounds like life and it gives us all something to smile over while we spend the next three minutes listening to this song, the one that Thomas Andrew wrote for Mahalia Jackson in 1937, and now this song has made its way through countless recordings by other people — Red Foley in '51 and then Tennessee Ernie Ford and Johnny Cash and Willie Nelson and Ronnie Milsap and Doc and Merle Watson and Randy Travis and the Avett Brothers and Elvis Presley, of course. You know that version.

And maybe that's how we all know the words to this song, because even if we've never thought about it before, this is one of those songs that's just always been around, the same way we think so many things have just always been around, and don't ever seem to change or go away, like this church meetinghouse, which has been here in Archdale since 1925, and Kepley's Barbecue in High Point, where we'll eat later, along with a slice, back at the house, of my mother's pound cake, which was my grandmother's recipe, a favorite that's just been around forever, and like my family, these people who are sitting beside me now and who have been in my life for as long as I've had a life, and now we're to the part where "the beasts from the wild shall be lit by a child," and there's the final refrain and then the song is over, and it hits me that I sure would like to hear it all again, just one more time. *Os*

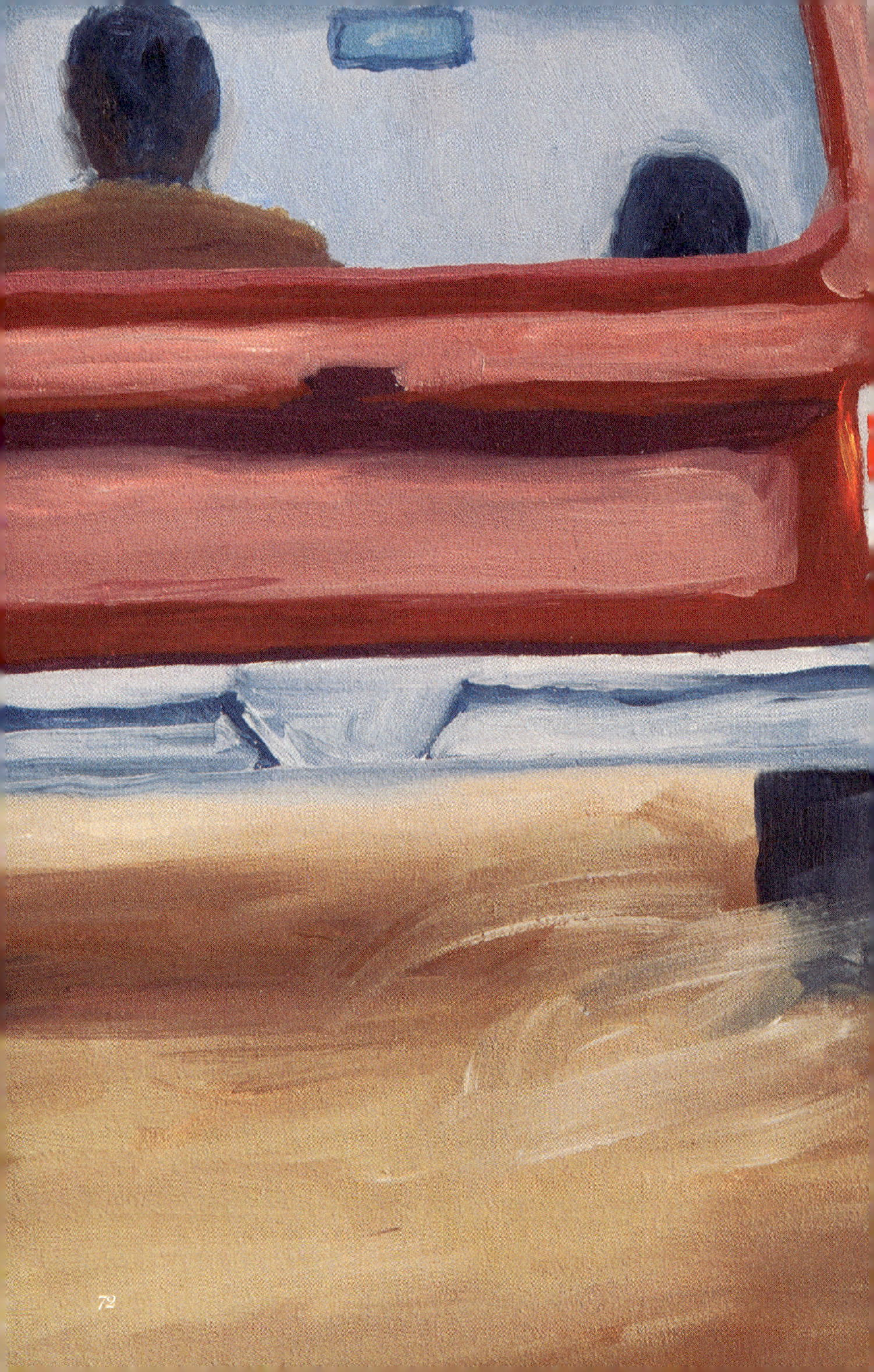

Something
in the Air

Messages from childhood are carried on the breeze.

I was in Edenton for a few days, and I drove over to Nixon Fishery on Rocky Hock Road. Four women stood at a cleaning table, scaling and filleting the daily catch. Mounds of silvery flounder and snapper and grouper slid across their table, and the four women worked in unison, slicing their knives across the bellies of those fish, scraping and cutting and discarding and packing, working fast, and laughing and talking cheerily to each other, not one of them noticing the overwhelming smell of brine and fishiness that permeated the air, the smell that nearly knocked me over when I walked in the door, that pungent, salty smell so essential to life in eastern North Carolina — clean, but sharp and bracing if you're not used to it.

It made me think about how desensitized we get to the smells that define a place, how quickly we stop noticing the aromas — sweet, citrusy, piney, honeyed, salty, woodsy, smoky, peaty — that give character to where we live.

But then, unexpectedly, you catch a hook of something that sends you straight back, to places long gone, and there you are

The smell of a coming rainstorm, of mist and damp earth, sends you running back home.

… 6 years old and pinching honeysuckle off a vine with your small fingers, and your grandmother is there, too, crouching down to show you how to delicately pull the string out, how to suck the tiny pool of sweet liquid out of the end, and she's close enough that you get a whiff of Ivory Snow detergent and Jergens hand lotion

74 SOMETHING IN THE AIR

... and then something else catches, and there you are again, 8 years old and in the back of your daddy's red pickup, the smell of his Pall Mall Gold wafting back from the driver's window. He's going slow, bumping along a dirt road, a joyride, keeping his eye on you in his rearview mirror. The tires kick up a cloud of chalky orange dust, and the smell of red clay and country trails the truck all the way home, and then, as you're about to bound out of the back, he's there to lift you up, swing you safely over the side, and off you go

... salty and sweaty and running wild on grass that's been warmed all day by the sun and smells like summer and freedom, and then

... there you are, deep in the woods, drawn by the promise of a creek, but that scent of sweet bubby, a bush you smell long before you see it, is just too much to take, and so you abandon the creek and your rocks and your stick pile, and scramble off in search of those deep purple buds giving off such sweet perfume that you can't believe they're not edible

... and then the smell of a coming rainstorm, of mist and damp earth, sends you running back home, and finally there you are again, standing in the kitchen, and there are hot biscuits on the table for supper and a pound cake on the counter and an icy tub of Cool Whip with sliced white peaches that smell like roses, and even though it's now and not then, if you close your eyes and keep breathing in, everyone you've ever loved will fill that kitchen, too: aunts and uncles and cousins and parents and grandparents, everyone standing around, talking and laughing cheerily to each other, not one of them noticing the smell of sugar and vanilla and butter and warmth and love and happiness, because, really, how do you even describe such a thing, these sensory memories so essential to our lives and our hearts, so overwhelming and meaningful when they come back. *Os*

Our Season *of* So Much

Thanksgiving Day, 1970s, have you ever seen so much food in all your life?

Coffee — there's always coffee — steams in the Corningware percolator on the stove, and on the kitchen table, there are deviled eggs, cold from having just been taken out of the refrigerator, a hulking avocado-green model, along with the relish tray, sectioned for the pickled beets and homemade vinegar dills that my grandmother put up in the summer. The electric can opener whirs now on a can of Ocean Spray cranberry sauce, the kind with the cranberries still suspended in the jelly, and someone opens the oven door and starts moving out a procession of metal sheet pans, one by one — Thanksgiving dressing. Never stuffing. I never once heard the word "stuffing" until I was older and ate dinner at a friend's, whose mother had made something called Stove Top.

This dressing, moist and golden with celery and sage, is covered in tinfoil, and someone peels back a corner and cuts a few squares with a butter knife, and we all come running, picking our piece and shoving the dressing into our mouths like we haven't eaten in days.

There are towering biscuits, flaked with White Lily, and a bowl of white beans next to a bottle of ketchup, because my dad and my grandfather like them that way, and there are green beans and creamed corn and candied sweet potatoes, caramelized and a little burnt, and mashed potatoes and a broccoli casserole that one of my cousins brought because, well, someone worried that there might not be quite enough food.

There's a turkey, carved with an electric knife; a mountain of white meat on one side of the platter, a pile of dark meat on the other, and there are pies — sweet potato and pumpkin, a container of Cool Whip set out to thaw on the countertop, and a baked persimmon pudding, its silky top oily and glistening.

Have you ever in all your life seen so much?

The television in the living room, a console Zenith, plays the Macy's Thanksgiving Day Parade, and later, there'll be a football game on, and kitchen chairs will migrate to the living room and ottomans will be rearranged, and the swing on the front porch will get claimed by someone, and this house will feel like it's overflowing, bursting with people, and what's happening now is that my grandmother is moving from room to room, gathering up all these people — her family, her kin, her children, her grandchildren. She holds on to one of our hands, and we let her steer us through the threshold, toward the dining room, listening to her beautiful, Southern, gentle voice chiming, "OK, everybody, let's eat," and what she really means is OK, everybody, let's be together, let's be family, let's talk and laugh and look at each other and smile and raise our glasses and lift our hearts and, on this day, today of all days, let's just be full. *Os*

Change Gonna Come

Every evening at dusk, a herd of white-tailed deer graze in the field across the street from my house. I spot them when I go out for my walk, and although I try not to disturb them, they spot me, too, lifting their heads from their dinner, staring, silent, motionless. I've seen a buck, a doe, a fawn. A family.

Their nightly routine doesn't seem too different from my own: a meal around 7, and some meditative gazing into the darkness before ambling back into the shadows of the woods.

There are still some woods here, a small patch of suburban forest thick with pine and oak and ferns, but this forest won't be here long. A new road is coming, part of Greensboro's Urban Loop, a six-lane freeway that'll circle the city. The road will run right next to my house and through those woods. Through the deer's habitat, too.

I'm not thrilled about this — I'm

sure those deer aren't, either; nobody wants a highway cutting through their backyard — but there are roads all over this state, and they have to go somewhere, right? *A change is gonna come,* sang Sam Cooke when he released that knock-you-to-your-knees song during Christmas week in 1964. The same year The Beach Boys did their Christmas album. The same year Dylan put out "The Times They Are a-Changin'." It seems 1964 was a year for change. Maybe every year is a year for change.

And maybe I shouldn't, but I can't help thinking about the idea of change at Christmastime, the season that embodies, paradoxically, no change at all, but just the opposite: Tradition. Custom. Ritual.

That's what we love about Christmas, right? The comfort in knowing our traditions enable us to hold on to the way things were.

FOR YEARS, AT CHRISTMAS, MY GRAND-mother rolled boiled cocoa between her fingers, the makings of her chocolate fudge, the old-fashioned, crumbly kind. For years, our three needlepoint Christmas stockings dangled from the mantel — my mom's, my dad's, and mine. On Christmas morning, when we turned those stockings upside down, I could count on bubble gum and a pack of in-the-shell peanuts. For years, a Smithfield pork shoulder warmed in the oven, and there were hot biscuits and potato salad and deviled eggs and sweet potatoes, always.

For years, there was a Belk box under the tree, put there by my dad for my mom, and in it, Estée Lauder Youth-Dew dusting power. For years, there were toys under the tree for me: a wooden boomerang, finger paints, Mad Libs, an egg of Silly Putty, a chemistry set, a typewriter. For years, my mom swagged doorways and tabletops with artificial greenery, decorations she and my dad bought 50 years ago.

So much has changed.

My parents don't exchange presents now; they haven't for years. They sold most of their decorations, an effort to pare down. I can't remember the last time I opened a toy. And what I wouldn't give to see my grandmother cutting squares of that fudge.

But here's this: There are still Neese's sausage balls on a plate in the kitchen, the way my mom has made them all my life; there's still my dad's favorite children's book, *The Night Before Christmas*, 70 years old with a tattered red spine, propped on the hearth. There are still the three of us on Christmas morning. A family.

One day, the road will be built. Those deer will graze somewhere else. Things will be different.

But until then, this season, let us celebrate the gift of the known. Let us praise what is left of the familiar. Let us hold each other's hands and be not afraid of the change that's gonna come. *OS*

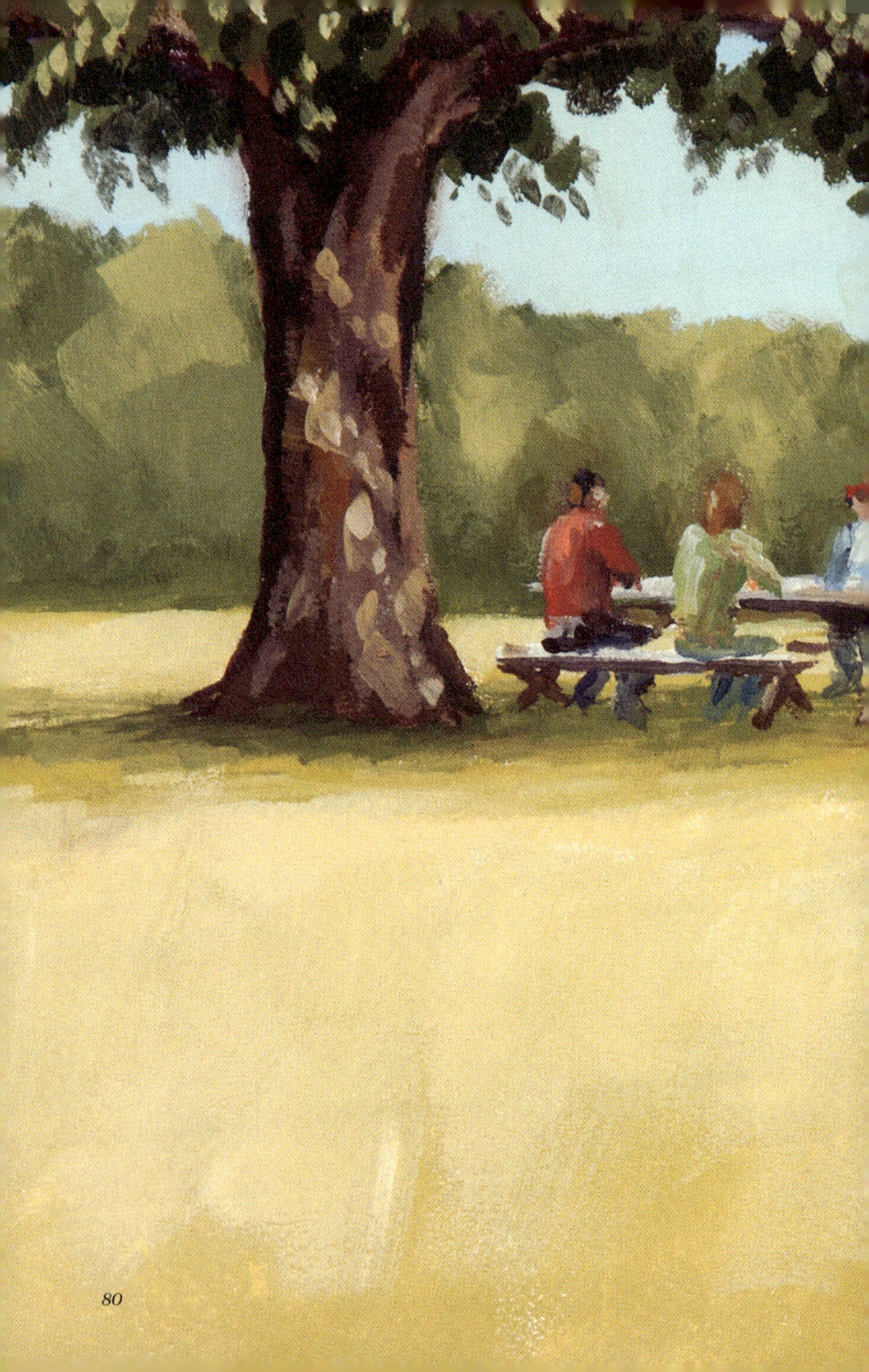

Everybody Talks About It

It's not just the heat.

Here is a one-room schoolhouse, built in 1903 and moved from a small community called Fountain to the Eastern Carolina Village and Farm Museum in Pitt County. It's a neat place, with 18 structures spanning a hundred years, from 1840-1940. In the schoolhouse, small wooden desks for younger grades sit up front; larger desks for the older students are in back.

Here's a country store from around 1879, and a corncrib and a milk house and a pigeon house and an outhouse and a log tobacco barn from the 1890s.

Here is a pecan tree. It's on the grounds, too, farther away from all the historic buildings at the village, and I know I'm supposed to be listening to the volunteer talk about these historic buildings, but the heat index for Pitt County today is 107 degrees — no, that's not a mistake — and Lord, I'm hot.

We're all hot. The backs of the shirts of everyone who's sitting in this one-room schoolhouse are soaked through. Joanne Honeycutt, a retired schoolteacher herself, is giving a wonderful overview of life in a North Carolina village, pre-air-conditioning, pre-World Wars I and II, even, but self-preservation is about to kick in, and I'm eyeing the shade of that pecan tree through the window and watching the breeze move those leaves just a little bit, and Joanne is swabbing her neck and cheeks and upper lip with a tissue. "I'm a dripper," she says, laughing, and we all are, what with this heat, my God, how did it get to be this hot in eastern North Carolina, and how in the world did anyone ever stand it back then, in one-room schoolhouses where the students generated enough body heat to raise the temperature another 20 degrees? How did anyone stand to work in these fields in this heat, priming tobacco, picking corn, harvesting potatoes? How did anyone cook in a kitchen, on an open fire? How did anyone make it through the summer?

Here is a log church, Primitive Baptist. The pews, original to a church that was built in the late 1700s, show a dark line of demarcation about two feet up from the floor. "From The Flood," Joanne says, the great flood, the 500-year flood, from Hurricane Floyd in 1999, when much of eastern North Carolina was devastatingly, shockingly, underwater.

> "But we survived. We weathered that flood."

Joanne kneels down and traces the flood line with her finger. "But we survived," she says, head nodding, sweat rolling down her face. "We weathered that flood."

Weathered.

The weather is hot. It's more than 100 degrees, and I think if we could just get out to that pecan tree, the one with the limb span so wide that surely it's been here for a century, then we'd be able to make it through this day. We'd get a break; we'd be a little less beaten down by the weather.

We weather hardships: storms, floods, heat.

We weather disease and sickness, heartbreak and loss.

We weather wars.

We weather the passage of time.

The hottest temperature ever recorded in North Carolina occurred in exactly this month — August — on the 21st in 1983 in Fayetteville, a temperature of 110 degrees. Beaufort County isn't far behind that record, 108 degrees in 1921. We've weathered these days before.

Here is a picnic table beneath the pecan tree, and I don't want to be rude, but I make a break for it, and everyone follows. And here, then, is respite, the way North Carolinians have always found it — in the shade of a tree, in the shadow of a church, in the shelter of family — a reminder that on hard days, there is always, eventually, hopefully, the promise of relief. *OS*

a Year *of* Firsts

There are the ones I wrote that were easy — about how he met my mother over a beer at the Matador Room in Greensboro and about his photography studio in High Point and about the foot-long hot dogs he grilled at his sandwich shop in downtown Asheboro.

There are the ones I didn't write, about how he had rheumatic fever as a boy, about how he hitchhiked to Chapel Hill to go to college, about how we went to Pinewood Country Club on Friday nights for steak and shrimp cocktail and Shirley Temples for me, about how he worked the crossword puzzle — in pen — every morning and showed me that "jai —" and "Harvard rival" always turn up as clues, about how he made lists for everything, his handwriting tall and precise and architectural.

There are the ones I wrote that were hard — about the selling of his beloved red pickup; about the aging of our old beagle, Muffin; about my parents' move from our family home. About cancer in his lungs.

He read all of these columns, the ones that were easy and the ones that were hard, and he rarely said anything about them to me, although I've learned that he also tore them out of this magazine, every last one of them, and saved them in a folder, along with recipes he wanted to make.

I don't know why this makes me smile, but it does: my columns tucked in with his plans for chicken pie.

ON THE LAST DAY OF HIS LIFE, I WALKED into the hospital room where my dad sat upright in bed, his face covered by an oxygen mask but his eyes open and alert. "Elizabeth's here," my mom said. He looked at me — his brown eyes are my brown eyes — and winked.

In that moment, my dad said everything to me without saying a word, all contained in one brief movement of an eye, and this month, I'm saying it all back, the only way I can, one word after another, 560 of them, in my 81st column for this magazine and, for me, the hardest one yet. The one that has one less reader.

For my mom and me, this will be our year of firsts. We'll get through our upcoming days by taking care of each other and marking the milestones, and I'm trying to believe that a year of firsts is better than a year of lasts.

Before my dad died, my mom tore off a square sheet from the day-by-day calendar hanging on the wall in his hospital room. A future page, one that was several days ahead. On the back of that calendar page, she wrote, "Happy Birthday, love Mom." Then she put the pen in my dad's trembling hand and held the piece of paper for him while he scrawled a message to me.

"Love, Dad."

On my birthday two days later — two days after he died — my mom gave me that calendar page. She'd been looking ahead.

My dad was an optimist. He was a list maker and a planner and a dreamer. At the beginning of every new year, in anticipation of whatever was to come, he wrote on a chalkboard that hangs in the hallway: "Going to be good!"

Even in our heartbreak, my mom and I can't help but believe that's true. *Os*

the Perfect Plate

Oh, Lord, how many times in my life did I eat at the late, great Blue Mist Bar-B-Q restaurant on U.S. Highway 64 between Asheboro and Ramseur, on Saturday afternoons, when the wood cooker out back spewed plumes of smoke — that blue mist — over the top of the building? Maybe 100 times? Maybe 200 times?

How many times did I slide into a window booth next to my grandparents, next to my parents, or next to my best friend from high school when we finally got bored cruising a one-mile stretch of Fayetteville Street on weekend nights and decided, simply, to just go get ourselves a sandwich?

How many times did I squirt sauce from a squeeze bottle, mash down a steamed bun, scoop up spilled slaw with a plastic fork, dip a hush puppy into ketchup, wad up a square of wax paper, and drain a Styrofoam cup of sweet tea?

BLUE MIST OPENED IN 1948 AND CLOSED in 2013, and for as long as I lived in Asheboro, it was *our* barbecue place, just like your place may have been A&M in Mebane, or Whitley's in Lexington, or Old Hickory House in Charlotte. Was it the best? I don't know. It was good. Or at least, it was good to me.

Yes, I know. East or west. Whole hog or pork shoulder. Tomato or vinegar. The feud has been going on for a long time. We've written about it. Heck, *everybody's* written about it. A few months ago, *The New Yorker* published a 4,000-word treatise on what constitutes "real" North Carolina barbecue. *National Geographic* loved our barbecue so much, it proclaimed a place in Ayden as having the best barbecue in the world.

In the *world*.

An Internet search for "North Carolina barbecue" brings up 1.1 million entries. These days, newspaper columns, radio commentators, Internet articles, and barbecue experts all over the place are telling you that *your* place, the one you've been going to all your life, is the best. Or maybe it's the worst. These days, other people are making those decisions.

Which brings me to a revelation: For all those years I ate at Blue Mist, I don't remember anyone talking about these things. Nobody went on quests to find The Perfect Plate. Nobody made Barbecue Bucket Lists. Nobody talked about whether the meat was smoked over wood or not (although to be fair, I guess it all was). I never heard anyone pledging allegiance to a certain style. We all just ate what was served in the restaurant down the road. We liked it. It was all good to us.

Back then, our barbecue joints weren't landmarks. They were just places in our towns where we went for lunch.

I'm glad the rest of the world has caught on to the fact that we have something good here. But I worry that the celebration has given way to criticism. That in finding ourselves in the midst of this Great Barbecue Debate, we've lost what it means to slide into a window booth somewhere and just, simply, eat.

Every couple of weeks, on doctor days, my mom drives her mother, my Grandma Dot, to Country Barbecue in Greensboro. It's something for the two of them to do together, and they order the same thing every time. Chopped sandwich. Hush puppies. Sweet tea. They don't talk about barbecue. They don't have to. This has been *their* place for a long time. They already know it's good. *O*

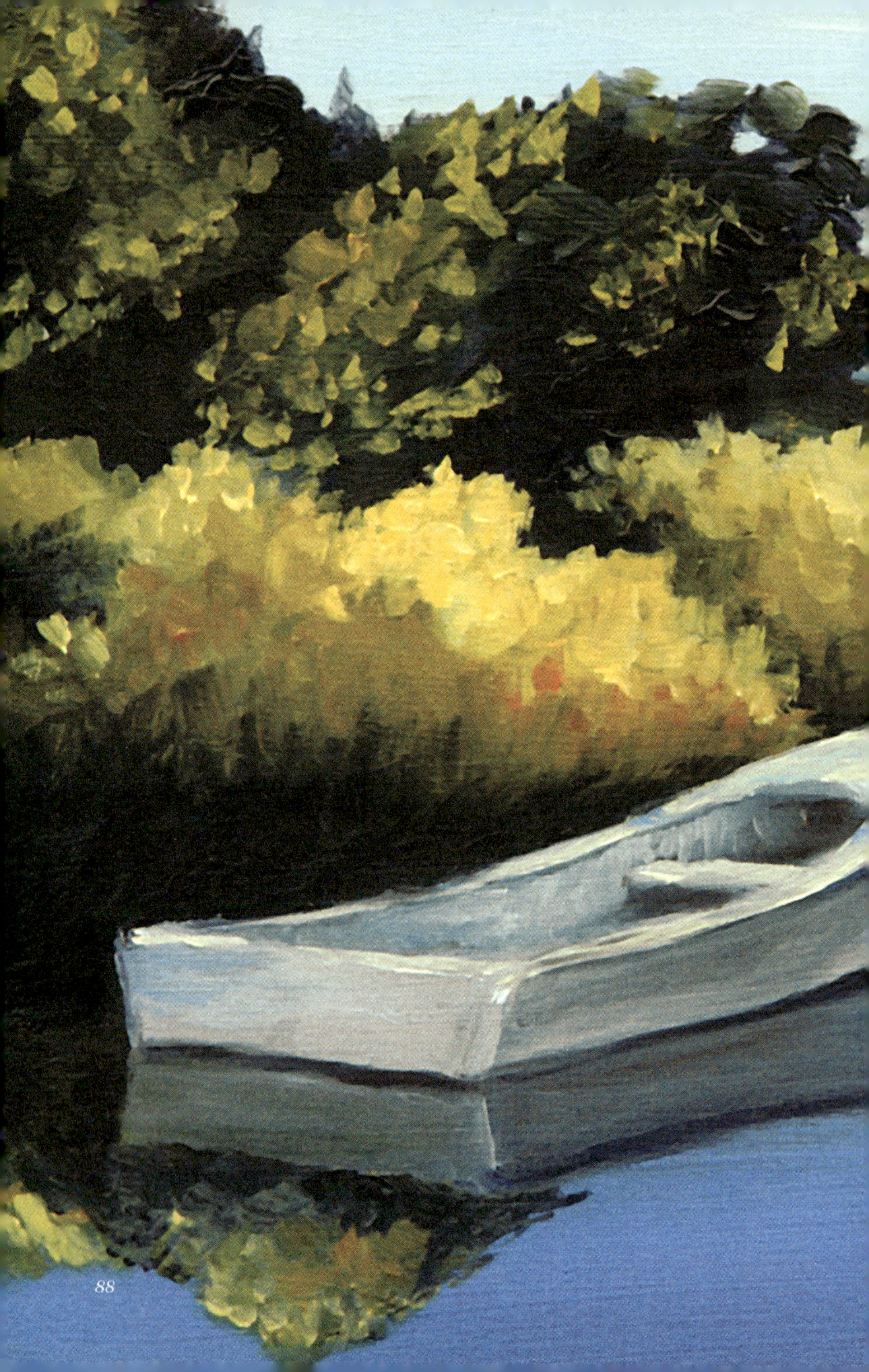

Beside *the* Still Waters

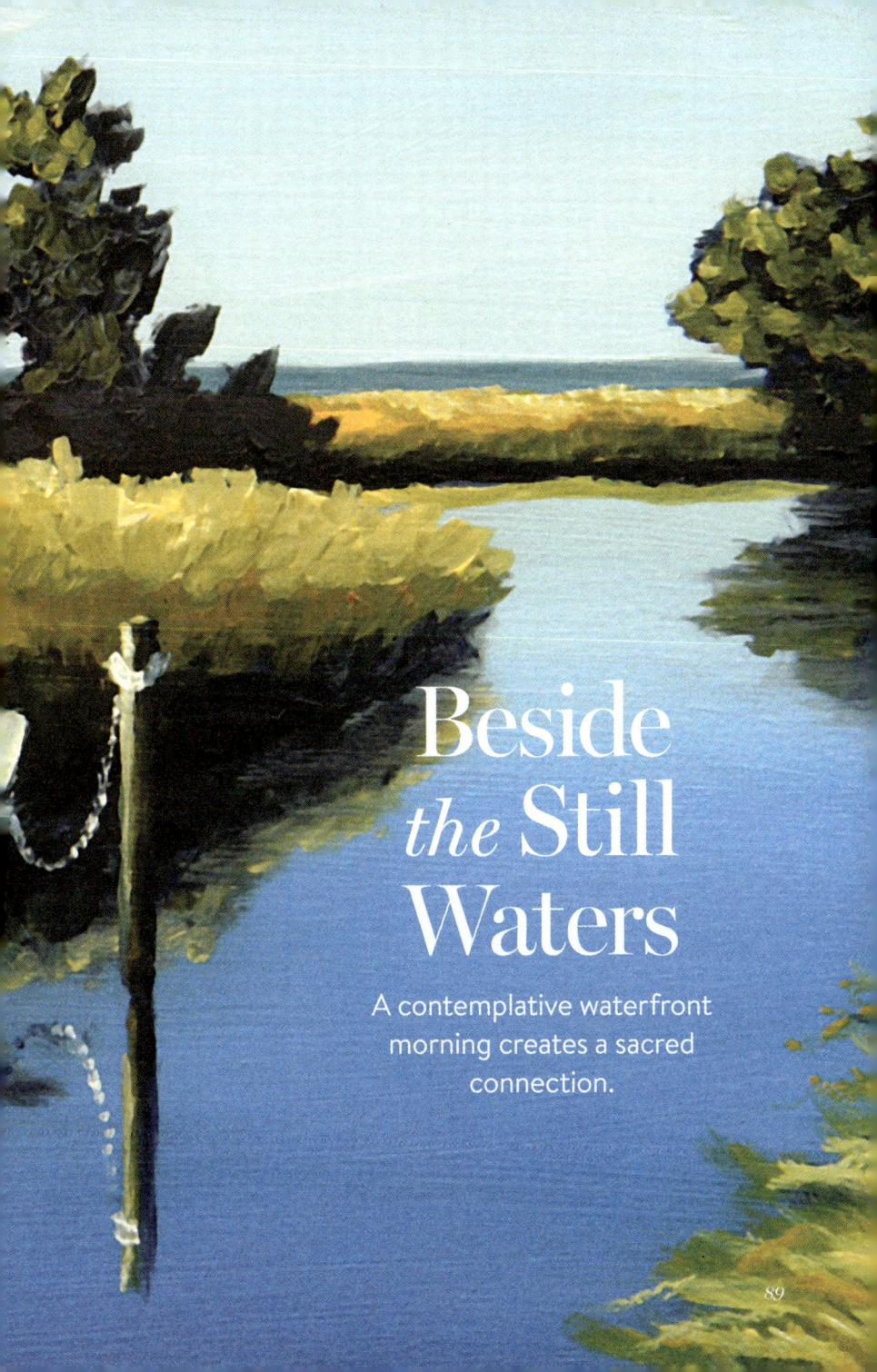

A contemplative waterfront morning creates a sacred connection.

A clear and peaceful Sunday morning on the waterfront in Washington and the boats are quiet in their slips, their bows gently rising and falling with the slightest waves on the Pamlico River. The two-seater swings overlooking the docks are empty, too, swaying as if someone has just risen and walked away. Bill's Hot Dogs on Gladden Street is closed on Sunday, but when you pass by on your way to service at First Presbyterian next door, you catch a whiff of onions, an aroma of that spicy chili hanging in the air, and right now, you can't think of a better place to be.

FIRST PRESBYTERIAN — BUILT IN 1823, rebuilt in 1867 after the Civil War — is one of a dozen churches in downtown Washington, each within walking distance of one another. This one has a full congregation today, all of us settling into our seats in the pews, turning to one another to talk, and someone named Barbara, retired here from Indiana, gives me — a visitor — the warmest smile.

"This is the day that the Lord has made," starts the service, and then the children in the congregation, six of them, go forth and sit on the floor in a semicircle in front of the pulpit, their fidgety bodies so full of life, bobbing and swaying as Alida Sawyer kneels down with them to deliver the children's message.

She holds up a sponge.

"Does everyone know what this is?" she asks, and the little heads bob up and down, and she passes the sponge around for the children to hold and touch, and she points out that the sponge is hard, rigid.

Then she takes the sponge and dips it into a bowl of water, holds it up, and asks the children what just happened when she dipped that sponge into water. A sea of tiny voices rises up — the children are calm now — and they chime, "It got softer," and Alida nods and says, "Yes, that's right. Water softens hard things."

ALIDA'S VOICE IS LIKE WATER, SO SLOW and soothing — she taught exceptional needs students in Beaufort County for 32 years — that everyone's shoulders drop a few inches, as if we, too, have been softened, as if that water has washed right over us, here in this church in Washington, after all, and never have I been more sure of something: the truth that water, more than anything else, holds the power to ease.

Alida says that water is mentioned in the Bible 722 times, and I think of all the places in North Carolina where I've noticed water, too, and have stood beside it and waded in it, and have swum in it and boated in it and scooped it into my hands and dipped my ankles in it, and have, every single time, come away feeling better than before I arrived at that water, every time uplifted.

How lucky we are to be reminded of what a small and connected part we all are in this cycle — now as it has been forever — of water that falls and then evaporates up into the sky, and we wait until it comes back to earth to cleanse us all over again, to lower our shoulders, to alleviate the hardness, to soften our hearts. *Os*

how to Collect *a* Life

I grew up around old things. A cast-iron scale from the 1800s sat on a wooden pedestal beside our front door. Advertising thermometers — "Drink Tru-Ade," "Chew Mail Pouch," and "Gulf No-Nox Gasoline" — covered our wood-paneled den walls. Something from another era was on display in every room: an oak hall tree from the '20s; Jugtown pottery from the '30s; metal Coca-Cola bottle carriers from the '40s.

My parents started collecting antiques in 1972, when I was 2. Most of the things I remember are gone now — sold when my parents finally downsized. My mother kept only a few pieces, and one of those was the first item she ever bought, the thing that ignited her 40-year love for antiquing: a metal, three-foot-tall, child's riding horse.

SHORTLY AFTER MY PARENTS GOT MAR- ried, my dad suggested that my mom go to the YWCA in High Point to learn to play bridge. He was a golfer, and he wanted her to have something to do in the clubhouse with the other wives.

At the Y, she noticed a white-haired woman sitting on a bench outside one of the classrooms. She held a metal stick in her right hand; with her left, she looped yarn around the stick, making a pattern.

"Crocheting," the woman said, when my mom asked what she was doing. "I'm teaching a class in a few minutes; why don't you stay for it?"

"I'm here to learn how to play bridge," my mom said.

"Psshh. You don't want to learn how to play bridge. Come on in here."

And so kicked off a lifelong friendship between my mother, then 22, and Mrs. Leo Kidd, well into her 60s.

Mrs. Kidd lived in a nice neighborhood in High Point called Emerywood. My mother visited every week, and Mrs. Kidd taught her something new — how to knit, cross-stitch, needlepoint.

Mrs. Kidd kept sourdough starter in her refrigerator for fresh bread and always had hors d'oeuvres on the counter. She filled her home — and her life — with things that delighted her, and she encouraged my mother, who was just starting to build a life, to do that, too.

One Saturday, while the two of them were shopping, my mom spotted the old metal horse in the corner of a store. It wasn't for sale. But she couldn't stop looking at it.

I don't know what drew my mother to that horse. The color? The style? That it reminded her of childhood? That it was discovered while on a happy outing with a friend? That it simply filled her with delight? Surely there's a certain serendipity that draws us to the objects that come into our lives — and to the people who come into our lives, too. If we can find a way to hold on to these objects long after the people have gone, maybe we should do that.

Somehow my mother convinced the store owner to sell the horse — the first time she'd ever bought anything like that — and she and Mrs. Kidd loaded it into the back of my mom's VW Bug, and she drove it home. There was no question it ended up exactly where it belonged. *OS*

Glass Half Full

Maybe you remember the spring out behind the house, with a metal dipper laid on top of a stump, the water so cold it'd make your teeth ache. Back at the house, a well bucket sat on the kitchen table with another dipper hooked to the side. Everybody in the family drank out of the same dipper.

Maybe you remember the wide-mouthed glass jars on the top shelf of the refrigerator, filled with sweet cow's milk, three inches of cream floating on top, Granny saying to the children, "Stir that milk," but the children never did, instead pouring their jelly glasses full of rich cream.

There was always buttermilk.

There was always tea.

I was 20 years old before I ever heard the phrase "sweet tea," said to a waitress at the Little Dipper in Asheboro by my friend who'd gone out of state to college.

We ate chicken pie, and she ordered a "*sweet* tea," as if there were any other kind, and it was the first time I'd ever considered the notion that tea might come unsweetened somewhere else.

Maybe you remember breaking from the tobacco fields at 10 in the morning, heat already spiking toward 90 degrees, and heading to the pickup with the cooler set out on the tailgate. Someone standing in the truck bed handed out drinks, tossed you a Cheerwine or a Dr Pepper, and you took your honey bun or your Royal Cake cream-filled oatmeal cookie to the shade of a tree and sat on the ground and stared off across the field and lifted that icy drink to your lips, sheer relief, nothing ever tasting so good in your life.

And then the farmer barked, "Pour 'em out and let's get it!" and everybody chugged their drinks and tossed the empties back into the cooler and went back to work.

Maybe you remember playing American Legion baseball; after a game in Randolph County, you slid into the booth at the Dixie Burger in Ramseur — baseball players got free food — but your mouth was still dry from kicking up all that red dirt on the field, and nothing beat that first, long swig of a cold Pepsi, all syrup and sweetness and pure *summer*.

And there were the country stores — Van Lanier's in Asheboro or the Grease and Run in Julian — where you ran in, screen door slamming, and tipped back the lid on the hulking chest freezer, a blast of cold air smacking you in the face, and reached in for a bottle of grape Nehi or orange Crush, flicking the cap into the built-in opener and guzzling half the bottle before you made it to the cash register.

There was no talk of "diet."

Maybe you remember carrying bottles in their cardboard holders to the grocery store to cash in for a nickel deposit. On Saturday mornings, when my grandmother and I went to Food World, my job was to cart the bottles she'd placed in the floorboard to the bin at the front of the store.

I don't see people doing that anymore. The first two-liter hit the shelves in 1970, and after that, it seems that a lot of things went away, that we all dove into a world of plastic and artificiality.

For a while, anyway.

I now see younger people, families with children, sitting at the soda fountain at Brown-Gardiner in Greensboro; I've popped open an RC to go with my BLT at Merritt's Grill in Chapel Hill, and I've dug through 200 bottles at Corbett's in Cary to find an old-fashioned Moxie.

Everything comes back around, if we give it time. The well refills. *Os*

Douglas Hoover grew up in High Point and spent his childhood summers drawing at the kitchen table of his grandparents' house. He studied graphic design and advertising at Randolph Community College and now works as a full-time artist, exhibiting at shows and galleries across North Carolina. He divides his time between Archdale and Ocracoke. See more at douglashoover.com.

to order more

If you've enjoyed *How to Collect a Life*, think of your family members, friends, and coworkers who would enjoy it, too! Call the Our State Store at **(800) 948-1409**, or visit **ourstatestore.com**.